"This volume on the ministry of Jesus is a fitting climax to Dr. Varner's trilogy on Jesus the Messiah. Having written masterful works on His advent as well as His death and resurrection, Varner now writes an informative work on His life while on earth. What makes this book even more valuable are the chapters on the history and culture of the Jewish people prior to Christ's advent. He discusses Josephus, the men of Qumran, Moses, and Melchizedek for instance, giving us a more well-rounded understanding of the Jewish world Jesus encountered during His life. He has also taken selected events from Christ's three years of ministry and given us a snapshot of who He was and what He did. He is to be commended on the surprising depth of his work."

Thomas Halstead
The Master's University

"The issues addressed by Dr. William Varner in *Messiah's Ministry* relate to the credibility of Jesus' stunning claims concerning Himself. Throughout His ministry, Jesus claimed to be the Messiah/Christ and to be God come in the flesh (Matt 16:16; John 11:27; Matt 26:63; John 20:30–31). When Paul told them about the remarkable claims and accomplishments of the Nazarene, the Bereans "searched the Scriptures to see if these things were so" (Acts 17:11) and thus believed. You will be blessed to walk with Dr. Varner through some of those Old Testament Messianic anticipations which God used to impact the truth-seeking Bereans so long ago."

Dr. Douglas Bookman
Shepherds Theological Seminary

"The best way to describe this excellent work by Dr. Varner is to point out that these are highlight aspects of the Life and the Ministry of Yeshua (Jesus) the Messiah. There are two things which are quite unique to this work. First, he covers what many other similar books cover about the Messiah being a Prophet, Priest, and King. Some of the insights in these three categories, however, are still unique to him and are worthy of consideration and study. Second, here are some new emphases that most books on the Life of Messiah simply do not cover: backgrounds from the Hebrew Scriptures and a frame of reference from rabbinic theology prevalent in first century Israel which is what the Messiah had to interact with whether it came from the Pharisees or from the Sadducees or from the Herodians. This material provides additional perspective in understanding Messiah's person and work and points out the uniqueness of Dr. Varner's work. This work is highly recommended, and I encourage all to read this volume as well as the other two volumes in the trilogy."

Arnold G. Fruchtenbaum
Director of Ariel Ministries

Messiah's Ministry

Messiah's Ministry

Crises of the Christ

WILLIAM VARNER

Fontes Press

Messiah's Ministry:
Crises of the Christ

Copyright © 2021 by William Varner

ISBN-13: 978-1-948048-62-0 (hardback)
ISBN-13: 978-1-948048-61-3 (paperback)

All rights reserved. No part of this publication may be reproduced, stored in a retrieval system, or transmitted in any form or by any means—electronic, mechanical, photocopy, recording, or any other—except for brief quotations in printed reviews, without the prior permission of the publisher. Translations are the author's own, although influenced by the Legacy Standard Bible.

Book and prayer icons at the end of each chapter are made by Freepik from www.flaticon.com.

Fontes Press
Dallas, TX
www.fontespress.com

To

Todd Bolen

Colleague, lover of Israel, Bible Lands photographer,
all around scholar and friend

Contents

	Foreword	1
	Preface	3
1	What Is a "Messiah"?	7
2	Messiah as "the" Prophet	19
3	Messiah and Josephus	29
4	Messiah and the Men of Qumran	39
5	Messiah in Matthew	51
6	Messiah and Moses	59
7	Messiah in the Water	65
8	Messiah in the Wilderness	75
9	Messiah in the Hometown	85
10	Messiah and Women	95
11	Messiah and the Goyim	109
12	Messiah and the Madman	121
13	Messiah's Metamorphosis	127
14	Messiah and the Mystery Man	137
15	Messiah Jesus—Should Jews Believe in Him?	145
	Further Reading	153

Foreword

By dealing with the ministry of Jesus from His baptism to His transfiguration, *Messiah's Ministry: Crises of the Christ* fills a gap left in the Apostles' Creed, which skips from His birth to His death without so much as a word to fill that yawning gap. As a well-established scholar, the author William Varner explains to his readership of serious-minded lay people not only the Biblical texts dealing with the middle part of Jesus' ministry but also its Jewish background both in the Old Testament and in other Jewish literature of the New Testament period, such as the Dead Sea Scrolls and the writings of Josephus, a first-century Jewish historian. Accompanying this rich tapestry of explanations are stunningly magnificent color photos of Biblical sites that help readers visualize the events they are reading about. Rounding out the whole are basic bibliographies for further reading and prayers designed to lead readers into informed Christian witness and devotion and, if used in Bible study groups (as it should be), into mutual edification.

It is with confidence, then, that I recommend this book—and also with special pleasure in that William Varner teaches at my alma mater, The Master's University, which I attended 1950–1954 (then called Los Angeles Baptist College) and concerning which I carry the fondest of feelings. Of blessed memory, my teachers there—Milton Fish, Herbert Hotchkiss, Thomas Price, Samuel Fisk, Marchant King—would have heartily seconded my recommendation.

Robert H. Gundry
Professor Emeritus and Scholar-in-Residence
Westmont College

Preface

The Apostle Paul declares in Romans 10:4 that the Messiah is the goal of the Torah: "For Messiah is the end of the law for righteousness to everyone who believes." In John 5:46, Jesus argues that since the religious leaders do not believe Moses, they do not accept Him as the promised Messiah. "For if you believed Moses, you would believe me; for he wrote of me." Likewise, in Matthew 5:17 Jesus says, "Do not think that I have come to abolish the Law or the Prophets; I have not come to abolish them but to fulfill them."

In other words, the ministry of Jesus the Messiah is rooted and grounded in the Hebrew Scriptures. If we want to understand Him and His ministry, we must view it all in light of the

Old Testament Messianic promises and themes. That has been the heartbeat of the first two volumes in this "Messianic Trilogy" expounding the life and ministry of Jesus the Messiah from His incarnation (*Anticipating the Advent*) to His resurrection and ascension (*Passionate about Passion Week*). When my boss, Tom Halstead, was reading *Advent* he suggested that since I had now written on the beginning and the end of Jesus' life, I should now write on the middle part of His earthly ministry and complete the whole story! Hence this third volume, which is actually the second one in terms of the chronology of Jesus' life and ministry!

So what you have before you is a treatment of the events of Jesus the Messiah's ministry from His baptism to His transfiguration. Along the way are some chapters that introduce the reader to some of the Jewish background of the Messiah's ministry, such as what the Dead Sea Scrolls and Josephus wrote about Jesus or the Messiah in general. So while we will survey the Messianic context of Jesus' ministry, we will explore a number of other Jewish themes that will help us appreciate the context of His "Jewishness." I also have included at least one color photo of an appropriate Biblical site in each chapter (except ch. 1), courtesy of BiblePlaces.com.

Permit a brief word about the title and especially the subtitle of this book. While I prefer the title "Messiah" to "Christ," I did use the latter term in the subtitle for a couple of reasons. First, I simply liked the ring of the alliteration in the initial "C's." Second, more importantly the expression "Crises of the Christ" intentionally recalls a book by that title by G. Campbell Morgan. Long out of print, that book by the British preacher inspired me long before I began writing about Jesus' role as the "Christ" (i.e., the Messiah).

As was the case with my book *Passionate about the Passion Week*, I have included a number of photographs of sites in Israel. These images help the reader to see where these important events took place, as well as reading about them. Thanks to BiblePlaces.com for permission to use these high-quality photographs.

Finally, I should thank my wife, Helen, for proofing the manuscript and suggesting to me some good ideas.

While this book has a firm academic basis, I want us to worship Jesus with our hearts as well as to understand Him with our heads. To that end, each chapter often offers ways in which the Messiah can become more precious to the believer. I also recommend another book to read on the subject of the chapter and sometimes suggest a prayer related to its main theme. May this little volume bless your heart as it informs your head! This is a book from which you can learn, through which you can worship, and with which you can witness to others!

Chapter 1

What Is a "Messiah"?

I magine the following scene. It is a few days after the birth of a boy-child in Bethlehem. His parents want to record His birth so they head to the city hall and enter the office of records. A grumpy old guy is sitting behind a desk and says to them, "What is the kid's name and what are your names?" Joseph responds quickly. "Well his name is Jesus Christ and my name is Joseph Christ and my wife's name is Mary Christ." "No", you cry out! "That is crazy! Christ was not their last name!" And you are correct. But how many people use the name "Jesus Christ" as if "Jesus" was His given/first name and "Christ" was His family/last name? That silly story also points out that the word "Christ" is not a name but a title, and it also serves to introduce the meaning of "Christ" in the title of this little book. To understand it all, we must delve into the Hebrew and Greek behind those all-important words.

The term *Messiah* is a transliteration (a representation in English) of the Hebrew word *mashiach*, which means "anointed one." The Greek translation of that word is *christos* and it is utilized in both the Septuagint (the Greek translation of the Old Testament abbreviated as LXX) and the New Testament. From this Greek word comes the English title, Christ. The Hebrew verb and noun are primarily applied to three types of individuals in the Old Testament period: priests (Exod 28:41; Lev 4:3), kings (1 Sam 16:13), and prophets (1 Kgs 19:16; Ps 105:15). The idea of being "anointed" is that the person so anointed is consecrated and equipped to do a sacred task, i.e., to perform a special function in the theocratic program of Israel.

Some critical scholars deny that *mashiach* is ever used in the Old Testament of a personal messiah. Of its thirty-nine occurrences, however, at least nine describe some future *anointed one* in the line of David who would be Yahweh's king (1 Sam 2:10, 35; Pss 2:2; 20:6; 28:8; 84:9; Hab 3:13; Dan 9:25–26).

The doctrine of a promised messiah, however, is not limited simply to the term itself. The Old Testament hope of a Deliverer who would crush Satan's head (Gen 3:15) and be the means of blessing to all mankind (Gen 12:3) is described by a variety of terms. Some of these terms are *son* (Ps 2:7), *branch* (Zech 6:12, 13), *servant* (Isa 41–53), and *king* (Zech 9:9).

Regarding the exact number of promises about a future *Messiah*, there is a wide divergence of opinion. Rabbinical writings refer to 456 Old Testament passages used to refer to the Messiah and messianic times (Edersheim, *The Life and Times of Jesus the Messiah*, 710–41). One Christian scholar lists 127 personal messianic prophecies (Payne, *Theology of the Older Testament*, 667–68). The differences are due to the different ways in which the New Testament refers to the Old Testament promises. There are *direct* messianic prophecies (e.g., Micah 5:2; Zech 9:9); *typical* messianic prophecies, utilizing an immediate referent in the prophet's day which pointed to the ultimate referent (e.g., the sacrificial Levitical system); and *applications* of Old Testament concepts to the Messiah (e.g., the reference Matt 2:23 makes to the prophets saying: "He shall be called a Nazarene"). If we limit ourselves only to the *direct* messianic prophecies just mentioned, a conservative number of them would be around 65.

Some scholars have recently stressed that the Messiah also embodies the ideal Israel, fulfilling in His person and role that special calling which Israel as a people failed to fulfill. This is the theological concept of *corporate solidarity*, where both Israel and the Messiah can be referred to by the same terms, e.g., as *seed, son,* and *servant*. It is in His role as the suffering *servant* in Isa 40-53 that the Messiah would "fulfill" the role which Israel as Yahweh's *servant* was called to fulfill but did not because of their unbelief and sinful behavior.

The key to understanding the role of the promised Messiah, and also the main difference between traditional Jewish and Christian messianic views, lies in recognizing His dual role of suffering and reigning. While there are many passages that describe a glorious reign for the Messiah (Jer 23:5, 6; 30:1-10; Zech 14:3ff.), there are others that describe His rejection and suffering (Ps 22; Isa 53; Zech 9:9; 12:10; 13:5-7). The New Testament views the suffering and glory passages as fulfilled in Jesus' first and second comings respectively (Luke 24:25-27; 1 Pet 1:10-11).

From a theological perspective, the unique role of the Messiah is that He combines in His person and ministry the roles of the three different *messiahs* of the Old Testament theocracy— the prophet, the priest, and the king. It is interesting to note that there were individual Israelites who combined the roles of a priest and prophet (Ezekiel, Jeremiah), and one who served as both king and prophet (David). No unequivocal example can be found, however, of an Israelite who held the "offices" of priest and king at the same time. David may have acted as a priest in his relationship to the sacrificial worship but he did not hold the office of a priest. This consistent Old Testament pattern of avoiding one person being both priest and king at the same time was because only the Messiah could combine these two functions (Zech 6:12-13). Furthermore, the Old Testament expectation of an eschatological *prophet* (Deut 18:15-19) found its fulfillment in the Messianic priest-king (see John 1:21 and Acts 3:22–26).

If you ask a person to name the founder of Christianity, he would probably reply, "Jesus Christ." As was mentioned that title means "Jesus the Messiah." Therefore, when the Bible and someone today uses the phrase "Jesus Christ" they both are really saying "Jesus the Messiah." Below that title "Christ/Messiah" is a deep layer of rich meaning. In this chapter, even with the danger of repetition (for effect), we will consider in more detail the special roles of "anointed ones" in the Old Testament and how Jesus embodied those roles in His life and ministry.

There is no better way to view this subject than through the grid of His three-fold work as a "Prophet," a "Priest," and a "King." It will be seen that Jesus is also presented in this way in the New Testament—as the one who combines all three of these roles in His own person.

Messiah as Prophet

Elijah was commanded by the Lord: "Elisha ... you shall anoint to be prophet in your place" (1 Kgs 19:16). The prophets were often referred to as "my anointed ones" (Ps 105:15). Likewise, the Messiah came to this earth, not only to rule and redeem, but also to proclaim the truths about Divine revelation. This was His role as "prophet"—one who declared God's message. Moses, the greatest of the Old Testament prophets, predicted, "The LORD your God will raise up for you a prophet like me from among you, from your brothers—it is to him you shall listen" (Deut 18:15). We will learn more about that chapter later. It is important to note that this "prophet" must be from the "brothers" of Israel, emphasizing His Jewish ethnic origin. While some have seen this prophecy as having its fulfillment only in the order of prophets during Israel's subsequent history, the Jews in New Testament times were still expecting this eschatological "prophet." The Dead Sea Scrolls, dating from the "time between the Testaments" indicate that a group of deeply religious Jews at Qumran were still looking for this great "prophet." The Jewish leaders inquired of John the Baptist: "What then? Are you Elijah?" And he said, "I am not." "Are you the Prophet?" And he answered, "No" (John 1:21).

The apostles, however, understood the real identity of this prophet. Peter boldly applied the prophecy in Deut 18 to Jesus as this Prophet-Messiah in Acts 3:22, while Stephen did the same in Acts 7:37. Jesus was the "ultimate prophet," the one who perfectly fulfilled all of the prophetic ideals. No one spoke like He did— "He was teaching them as *one* having authority, and not as their scribes" (Matt 7:29). He announced His identity as the Messianic Prophet when He stood before His home synagogue and proclaimed, "The Spirit of the Lord is upon Me, Because He anointed Me to preach the gospel to the poor" (Luke 4:18a). While Psalm 22 concerns the priestly work of the Messiah in His sacrificial suffering, it also equates this messianic figure with that of the anticipated prophet who will faithfully declare God's word. "I will tell of (proclaim) your name to my brothers; in the midst of the assembly I will praise you" (Ps 22:22, cited in Heb 2:12).

Therefore, Jesus certified Himself as the promised Messianic "Prophet" by faithfully predicting events that took place just as He predicted. Only one example needs to be given. Jesus predicted the total destruction of the Jerusalem Temple (Matt 24:2–3). His prophetic prediction was fulfilled in AD 70, when the armies of Rome did just that. No one else in history qualifies to be the Prophet predicted by Moses. Jesus **is** that Messianic Prophet. (We will take a more in-depth look at Jesus as the Messianic Prophet in the next chapter.)

Messiah as Priest

Aaron and his sons, as Israel's priests, were the second class of ancient Israelites who were anointed with oil (Exod 29:7; Lev 4:3). One of the functions of the Old Testament priest was to offer a sacrifice. The Messiah's priestly function is seen both in his work as the *sacrificer*, who officiates at the altar, and also as actually becoming in His own person the *sacrifice*, the one who is slain to atone for sin!

The role of the Messianic Priest appears in three ways in the Old Testament scriptures. Psalm 110, quoted in the New Testament more than any other passage, states that David's "Lord" (i.e., the Messiah) is declared by Divine oath to be a priest: "Yahweh has sworn and will not change His mind, 'You are a priest forever according to the order of Melchizedek'" (Ps 110:4). The Book of Hebrews is a sermon expounding this great psalm and its promises of Messiah's priesthood, exaltation, and session at the Father's right hand. Jesus' being in the "Melchizedekan" priesthood is shown to be "better" than the temporary and mortal Levitical priesthood (7:11–28). The sacrificial act of the Messiah is also described in terms of Psalm 110 in Heb 10:12–14: "But He, having offered one sacrifice for sins for all time, sat down at the right hand of God, waiting from that time until His enemies are put as a footstool for His feet. For by one offering He has perfected for all time those who are being sanctified."

The second Old Testament passage that describes the priestly sacrifice of the Messiah is in that "Servant Song" called by many the clearest example of the Gospel in the Old Testament—Isaiah 53. After describing the suffering of the Lord's "servant," verse 10 declares, "when his soul makes an offering for sin." The word for "offering" is the Hebrew *asham*, which is used elsewhere in the Old Testament for the "trespass offering" (Lev 5:19). This marvelous acknowledgement of the Messiah's priestly sacrifice is then followed by the statement in verse 12 that "he makes intercession for the transgressors"—another priestly function.

One other passage mentions the priestly sacrifice of the Messiah: Dan 9:24–27. Space does not allow for a full treatment of the amazing chronological aspects of this passage. Suffice it to say that it prophesies, among other things, that "an anointed one (the Messiah) shall be cut off" (9:26). The verb used here (*karat*) is one that is used for violent death and "cutting the covenant" in many other Old Testament passages (e.g., Gen 15:18)—all clearly sacrificial language. The verse also states that this sacrificial death of the Messiah will take place before the Temple is destroyed in AD 70.

Sacrifice, offering, intercession—all these terms related to the anointed Israelite priests in the Old Testament are applied to the work of Jesus in the New Testament. Yes, in light of all this, Jesus is the Messianic Priest. (We will look more in-depth at this subject when we examine "Messiah and Melchizedek" in a later chapter.)

Messiah as King

The first king in Israel, Saul, was anointed by Samuel to initiate his role in the theocratic kingdom (1 Sam 10:1). Thereafter, even in his disobedience, he was the "Lord's anointed" or messiah (1 Sam 24:6). Saul's successor David was also anointed by Samuel (1 Sam 16:13). Thus, the king joined prophets and priests in Israel as "the Lord's anointed ones."

However, long before Saul and David, prophetic Scripture had anticipated an anointed king, one whose characteristics went beyond any earthly monarch. Jacob, around 1800 BC, and Balaam, around 1400 BC, prophesied of the King-Messiah as wielding the scepter, gaining the obedience of the peoples (Gen 49:10) and breaking down human opposition (Num 24:17). The concluding verse of Hannah's "Magnificat" then becomes the first passage in which the coming Deliverer is specifically designated as "Messiah" and also the first in which he is specifically called "King." "He will give strength to his king and exalt the power of his *anointed*" (1 Sam 2:10c). This future person cannot be either Saul or David for this king's reign takes place in that future age when the Lord shall judge the ends of the earth.

The Psalms are full of references to a future "king" whose characteristics make it clear that David, as powerful as he was, could only have been the typical prototype of the ultimate "King." David refers to the "King-Messiah" as the Son of God (Ps 2:2, 7). David also predicted Messiah's ascension to the right hand of "Yahweh" as David's "*Adon*" ("Lord," Ps 110:1). In the same psalm this one is described as "ruling" in the midst of his enemies after they have been defeated (110:4). Solomon also looked beyond his own time and foretold the coming of the perfect king whose kingdom would take up where his own had terminated: "May he have dominion from sea to sea, and from the River to the ends of the earth!" (Ps 72:8). In a similar fashion, Ps 45:6 addresses itself to the Divine Messianic King, saying, "Your throne, O God, is forever and ever. The scepter of your kingdom is a scepter of uprightness."

Isaiah predicted that the Messianic child would bear the governmental authority upon the throne of David (Isa 9:7). Micah, however, spoke of Messiah's birth in the humble village of David's royal family in Bethlehem, rather than in the royal city of Jerusalem (Micah 5:2). Jeremiah unites Deity and humanity when he describes the reign of King-Messiah: "Behold, the days are coming, declares the LORD, when I will raise up for David a righteous Branch, and he shall reign as king and deal wisely, and shall execute justice and righteousness in the land. In his days Judah will be saved, and Israel will dwell securely. And this is the name by which he will be called: 'The LORD is our righteousness'" (Jer 23:5–6). While most of these promises foresee the glories normally associated with the reign of a King, Zechariah reverts to a humble, royal description: "Rejoice greatly, O daughter of Zion! Shout aloud, O daughter of Jerusalem! behold, your king is coming to you; righteous and having salvation is he, humble and mounted on a donkey, on a colt, the foal of a donkey" (Zech 9:9). To balance these seemingly contradictory descriptions necessitates two comings of that King, first in lowliness (see Matt 21:5) and then in glory (see Rev 19:11–16).

Jesus' terms of kingship, however, would not be accepted by a Roman procurator's view of these matters. In answer to the straightforward question by Pilate, "Are you the King of the Jews?" (John 18:33), Jesus answered, "My kingdom is not of this world. If My kingdom were of this world, then My servants would be fighting so that I would not be delivered over to the Jews; but as it is, My kingdom is not from here" (John 18:36). Although grossly misunderstood by His accusers, it was for this crime that the Messiah was executed: "And Pilate also wrote an inscription and put it on the cross. It was written, "JESUS THE NAZARENE, THE KING OF THE JEWS" (John 19:19). Even as He was mocked, Jesus was the Messianic King.

In a later chapter, we will look at the beliefs of the Qumran authors of the Dead Sea Scrolls, who lived and wrote in the two centuries prior to Jesus. Their writings make it clear that they understood this three-fold role of the Messiah from the Hebrew Scriptures they so venerated. However, they thought that there would be three different Messiahs who would come in the last days: a Messianic Prophet, a Messianic Priest and a Messianic King. They were on the right track, although they did not have it completely clear. There was not to be three different messiahs, but one with three roles! Jesus' ministry and the way in which His followers believed in Him made it clear that He combined each of these normally separate roles in His own precious person and work. Consider a couple of New Testament passages in which the rubric of Jesus as "Prophet-Priest-King" makes the passage come alive to the reader. In Heb 9:24–28 the word "appear" occurs three times:

> For Christ did not enter holy places made with hands, *mere* copies of the true ones, but into heaven itself, now to *appear* in the presence of God for us; nor was it that He would offer Himself often, as the high priest enters the holy places year by year with blood that is not his own. Otherwise, He would have needed to suffer often since the foundation of the world; but now once at the consummation of the ages He has been manifested (*appeared*) to put away sin by the sacrifice of Himself. And inasmuch as it is appointed for men to die once and after this *comes* judgment, so Christ also, having been offered once to bear the sins of many, will *appear* a second time for salvation without *reference to* sin, to those who eagerly await Him.

Jesus "appeared" (v. 26) on earth in His role of "Prophet"; He "appears" (v. 24) now in Heaven in His role as "Priest"; He will "appear" (v. 28) at His second coming in His role as "King." Or consider John's description of the Messiah in Rev 1:5: "And from Jesus Christ the faithful witness (Prophet), the firstborn of the dead (Priest), and the ruler of kings on earth (King)."

There were individual Israelite examples of a person who was at the same time a priest and a prophet (Ezekiel, Jeremiah), and also a person who was at the same time both a king and a prophet (David). But no examples exist of an Israelite being both a priest and a king. As a matter of fact, whenever a king tried to serve as a priest he was punished severely (e.g., Saul: 1 Sam 13:8–14; Uzziah: 2 Chr 26:16–20). This restriction was because only the Messiah could combine these two functions in His own person. Hear the prophecy of Zechariah:

> Behold, the man whose name is the Branch: for he shall branch out from his place, and he shall build the temple of the LORD. It is he who shall build the temple of the LORD and shall bear royal honor, and shall sit and rule on his throne. And there shall be a priest on his throne, and the counsel of peace shall be between them both (Zech 6:12–13).

"A priest on his throne"—this is something that was unheard of in the Israelite economy of the Old Testament. It was not exemplified there because this dual role was only to be fulfilled by Israel's priest-king, Jesus the Messiah.

Therefore, the final *Messiah* would be the ideal prophet-priest-king, combining the role of the Prophet who declared God's will to man; the Priest, who offered a sacrifice to God for man; and the King who alone has the right to rule over man as God. As the anointed one of the Lord, Jesus was, is, and always will be the Prophet, the Priest, and the King. Each of these roles, however, was emphasized at different times in His ministry. During His earthly ministry of teaching and preaching, His role as *prophet* was in the forefront (see John 6:14; 7:40). His sacrificial death, resurrection, ascension, and current session at His Father's right hand brings His role as *priest* in view (Ps 110:1–2; Heb 4:14; 10:11–12). Following His return to earth, during His Millennial reign, His role as *king* will be stressed (Rev 19:16). He is always the anointed *king*, but He enters into His public office as *king* during the Millennium. An Old Testament example of this was the period of time between David's anointing as king (1 Sam 16:13) and his eventual enthronement as Saul's successor (2 Sam 5:3). In other words, from the time that David was anointed by Samuel, he was the new king, having replaced King Saul who had been rejected by God. It was not, however, until the Lord in His own time removed Saul that David publicly entered into his role as king. Therefore, the final *Messiah* would be the ideal prophet-priest-king.

Only a theology that includes a future kingdom with Jesus literally reigning over a renewed yet literal earth can enable one to fully appreciate the Messianic role of Him who is the "Hope of Israel." We may differ with sincere believers on how Jesus will manifest His future role as King. The fact, however, that He came as the "Messiah of Israel" in fulfillment of the Old Testament messianic hope is something that unites all believers. We all agree with Philip's excited statement to Nathanael: "We have found Him of whom Moses in the Law and *also* the Prophets wrote—Jesus of Nazareth, the son of Joseph" (John 1:45).

In light of all that has been seen of the "offices" of the prophet, the priest and the king in the Old Testament period, and in light of the amazing way in which Jesus fulfills all three roles, may we all conclude with the words of Andrew: "We have found the Messiah (which means Christ)" (John 1:41).

▼

Anyone writing on the life of Jesus is indebted to Alfred Edersheim, author of *The Life and Times of Jesus the Messiah*, 2 volumes, Eerdmans reprint, 1967. His Jewish background gave him a special expertise in the Messianic themes which are so crucial in writing a book like this one.

Almighty Father, who gave your only Son to die for my sins and to rise for my justification: Give me grace so to put away the leaven of malice and wickedness, that I may always serve You in pureness of living and truth; through Jesus the Messiah Your Son my Lord, who lives and reigns with You and the Holy Spirit, one God, now and forever. Amen.

(Adapted from *The Divine Hours*)

Chapter 2

Messiah as "the" Prophet

Leadership! It is a word that we hear constantly today. Leadership, however, is anything but a novel idea that moderns have discovered. It certainly is as old as ancient Israel. God provided chosen leaders to lead His chosen people.

As we have seen, there were three administrative offices given by the Lord God to Israel to rule over and guide them—the king, the priest and the prophet. The king ruled over Israel *for* God; the priest represented the people *before* God; and the prophet spoke to the people *from* God. Each one of these leaders was anointed with oil when he assumed his office as a king (1 Sam 16:3), or as a priest (Exod 28:41) or as a prophet (1 Kgs 19:16). Thus, each could be referred to as an "anointed one" or a "messiah" (*mashiach* in Hebrew) in the general sense of the term. While an individual could serve as both a priest and a prophet (e.g., Samuel, Jeremiah, Ezekiel), and one person might serve as both king and prophet (e.g., David), no Israelite ever combined in his own person the roles of priest and king. Those who attempted to do so were judged by God (e.g., Saul: 1 Sam 13:8–14; Uzziah: 2 Chr 26:16–20). Only the Messiah could serve as both priest and king

(Zech 6:12–13). The role of the prophet also would belong to *the* Messiah, thus combining all three of these normally separate offices of Old Testament Israel as the anointed Prophet-Priest-King.

Yahweh gave instructions regarding each of these offices in one extended section of the Book of Deuteronomy. In Deut 17:14–20, guidelines are given for the king of Israel—directions often disobeyed by subsequent kings who later reigned over Israel. In Deut 18:1–8, guidelines are given for the priests and the Levites, particularly regarding the portions of land and food belonging to them. Finally, in Deut 18:15–19, Moses provided the characteristics of *the* Prophet and contrasted Him with false prophets as well.

In the previous context (18:9–14) there is a stern warning against all sorts of occult practices—soothsayers, sorcerers, mediums, spiritists—all of whom are called an "abomination to the LORD" (v. 12). To express this in another way, this passage warns us first where we are *not* to get our information (from occult sources) and then tells us where the reliable source is—the Prophet raised up by God.

> The LORD your God will raise up for you a prophet like me from among you, from your brothers—it is to him you shall listen—just as you desired of the LORD your God at Horeb on the day of the assembly, when you said, "Let me not hear again the voice of the LORD my God or see this great fire any more, lest I die." And the LORD said to me, "They are right in what they have spoken. I will raise up for them a prophet like you from among their brothers. And I will put my words in his mouth, and he shall speak to them all that I command him. And whoever will not listen to my words that he shall speak in my name, I myself will require it of him. But the prophet who presumes to speak a word in my name that I have not commanded him to speak, or who speaks in the

name of other gods, that same prophet shall die" (Deut 18:15–20).

In this passage, Moses lists seven characteristics of this Prophet:

1. He must be *called by God* ("The LORD your God will raise up unto you a Prophet" v. 15). No self-ordained preacher could claim this role. He had to have the stamp of a divine call.

2. He must be an *Israelite* ("from among you, from your brothers," v. 15). Therefore, no Gentiles need apply for this job! The truth of this verse was the main reason Jews simply could not accept Muhammad as God's prophet—he was not Jewish!

3. He must be *like Moses* ("a prophet like me," v. 15). This, however, raises a problem. According to Deut 34:10 and Num 12:6–8, there never was a prophet like Moses—his experience with God was unique. We must then look beyond the Isaiahs and the Jeremiahs and the Malachis to discover one *like Moses*.

4. He must have the *authority* of a prophet (vv. 16–17). In other words, no uncertain sound was to be heard from him. Only "thus says the Lord" was to preface his message.

5. He must *be obeyed* ("to him you shall listen," v. 15; "and whoever will not listen to my words that he shall speak in my name, I myself will require it of him," v. 19). There was no option in obeying the Prophet's word—there was either obedience or judgment. Anyone who dared to disregard a prophet's message brought judgment on himself!

6. He must *speak only God's word* ("I . . . will put my words in his mouth," v. 18). He was not to offer his own opinions but to proclaim only the word of God. A prophet who spoke his own ideas would die (v. 20).

7. He must *certify himself* by tested prophecies. According to Deut 18:21–22, a false prophet could never *hit 1.000* (to use a baseball analogy)—he would eventually fail in his predictions.

Not so with the Lord's Prophet. His short-term prophecies would be attested by their accurate fulfillment. The true prophet's power came from the omniscient God who knows all things—past and present, actual and possible.

This passage made a deep impression on the Jews of the Old Testament and also on those who lived after the restoration from the Babylonian captivity. Although some rabbis desired to see this prophecy fulfilled in Joshua, Ezra, or Jeremiah, others knew that such was impossible because none of them was equal to Moses (see Num 12:6–8). Imbedded within the psyche of the people was a conviction that a Prophet would someday arrive like none who had ever appeared before in Israel's history. It was He who would be the fulfillment of Moses' description in this passage.

Consider, for example, how this expectation of *the Prophet* is portrayed in the Gospel of John. When representatives from Jerusalem were sent to inquire of John the Baptist, they asked him a number of questions about his identity. Note John 1:21: "And they asked him, 'What then? Are you Elijah?' He said, 'I am not.' 'Are you the Prophet?' And he answered, 'No.'" These priests were referring to the Prophet promised by Moses in Deut 18. While John recognized the importance of his own role, he knew that he was not *the Prophet* promised by Moses.

When Jesus instructed the Samaritan woman about the true nature of worship, she remarked, "I know that Messiah is coming (He who is called Christ); when He comes, He will declare all things to us" (John 4:25). Her concept of Messiah is very revealing, especially in light of the fact that the Samaritans only accepted the five books of Moses as their Scriptures. It was in one of these five books (Deut 18) that someone was promised who would declare the whole counsel of God. Jesus then identified Himself with the one she believed to be that revealer: "I who speak to you am *He*" (John 4:26).

Arab woman drawing water from Jacob's Well in Samaria. One of the most reliable Biblical sites; photo taken 1920 in the crypt of the unfinished church built around the well

On two occasions the crowds proclaimed about Him, "This is truly the Prophet who is to come into the world" (John 6:14; 7:40). They were clearly identifying Jesus with the promised one of Deuteronomy 18. In the infant days of the early Church, both Peter (Acts 3:22-24) and Stephen (Acts 7:37) saw in Jesus' life and ministry the fulfillment of Moses' prophecy.

Jesus fulfilled all seven of the characteristics of the prophet mentioned in Deut 18:15-19.

1. He was called by God (Luke 9:35);
2. He was an Israelite (Matt 1; John 1:49);
3. He was a mediator like Moses (1 Tim 2:5; Heb 1:1, 3);
4. He spoke with an authority unlike the teachers of His day (Matt 7:28-29);

5. His Father declared that His words must be obeyed (Matt 17:5);

6. He spoke the Word of God in God's name (John 12:8–49; John 5:45);

7. He certified Himself by miracles and prophecies which no one could deny (John 3:2; Acts 2:22).

If Jesus did not fulfill Moses' description of the Prophet, then no one has ever appeared who has, and Israel's hope remains unfulfilled. While various prophets arose throughout Israelite history, none could claim to even approach the level of Moses who had a face-to-face encounter with God. Num 12:6–8 is a Divine declaration of the absolute uniqueness of Moses' prophetic role:

> And he said, "Hear my words: If there is a prophet among you, I the LORD make myself known to him in a vision; I speak with him in a dream. Not so with my servant Moses. He is faithful in all my house. With him I speak mouth to mouth, clearly, and not in riddles, and he beholds the form of the LORD. Why then were you not afraid to speak against my servant Moses?"

But there was another who did function even as Moses did, but even in a greater role than that great Old Testament mediator. Listen to John's description of the Logos: "In the beginning was the Word, and *the Word was with God,* and the Word was God" (John 1:1). That same Word created all things (John 1:3) and is the source of life (John 1:4) and light (John 1:9). Furthermore, that Word became incarnate in the person of Jesus of Nazareth (John 1:4). To all who receive Him, He gives the authority to become children of God (John 1:12).

There were other ways in which the Messiah would be like Israel's great leader. Moses was a *redeemer* who brought God's people out of Egypt's bondage (Exod 3:10); Messiah is a redeemer who brings God's people out of sin's bondage (Isa 53:4–12). Moses was a *mediator* who went between God and Israel (Exod 19:16, 19); Messiah is a mediator between God and His redeemed (1 Tim 2:5). Moses was an *intercessor* before God for Israel (Num 14:11–20); Messiah intercedes for His followers before the Lord (Isa 53:12; Heb 7:25). The writer to the Hebrews exults in the fact that not only was Jesus like Moses, He was actually *greater* than Moses. While Moses was a servant *in* God's house, Jesus the Messiah was actually the Son over the house in which Moses was a servant (Heb 3:5–6). We look forward to seeing how Matthew presents the Messiah Jesus as a New Moses in the early chapters of his Gospel.

In Jesus, the Jewish person finds all that the Hebrew Scriptures describe as essential for life. As the anointed *King*, He has a kingdom in which to rule over willing subjects. As the anointed *Priest*, He is the sacrifice for our sins, and He intercedes for us in God's presence. As the anointed *Prophet*, He is the faithful voice of divine instruction. He is Messiah—Prophet, Priest and King—all in one ineffable person. Let us worship Him, adore Him and proclaim Him to Jews and Gentiles alike, for He meets the need of our hearts for time and eternity.

Louis Lapides is a Jewish believer who ministers in California and has become a dear friend. I remember reading years ago how the Lord used this passage to bring him to the Messiah. Here is a summarized account of his story, written to me in his own words.

* * *

"Moses is for Jewish people; Jesus is for Christians," was my smart aleck reply to a Christian asking whether I believed in Jesus. I was 22 years old, freshly returned from Vietnam. With two decades of life behind me including one year in Southeast Asia, I believed I knew it all. Eventually, a question came around I did not want to hear. The Baptist street evangelist doing the interrogation inquired, "Have you ever read your Bible?" "Sure," I replied. "I went to Hebrew school and we read the entire Torah." Next I was probed whether I had studied the Hebrew prophets. My examiner rattled off the names of prophets I never heard of: Micah, Zechariah, Zephaniah and Ezekiel. I was embarrassed. The next challenge floored me, "Would you be willing to read the Jewish Scriptures and ask the God of Abraham and Isaac and Jacob whether Jesus is the Messiah of Israel?" Little did I know my comment comparing Moses to Jesus would come back to haunt me.

As an avid reader of religious works such as Eastern philosophies, I figured scanning the Bible would be a cinch. I breezed through Genesis and caught God's promise to Adam and Eve in Gen 3:15 of a future, messianic figure who would defeat the power behind the evil serpent-Satan. Then in Gen 49:10 I understood the Messiah would come from the tribe of Judah. In addition, He would be a great ruler over Israel and the nations. I trekked my way through the thick forests of Exodus, Leviticus and Numbers. In Deut 18 I slammed into a prophecy that bewildered me. The Lord God instructed Moses that He would raise up a prophet in Israel like Moses. Deut 18:18 states, "I will raise up for them a prophet **like you** from among their brothers. And I will put my words in his mouth, and he shall speak to them all that I command him." Another Moses? One through whom God reveals His truth? A leader whose words God will hold His people accountable to obey? Look at Deut 18:19, "And whoever will not listen to my words that he shall speak in my name, I myself will require it of him." Who could this prophet be? It would be nearly impossible to miss someone as important as this coming One.

Then I started my journey through the New Covenant, I was still puzzled about the Deuteronomy 18 passage. Was it ever fulfilled? However, when I continued to look into the gospel accounts, I noted the first century Jewish community was still awaiting that Great Prophet. When the people witnessed the miracle of the feeding of the 5000, they remarked, "This is indeed the Prophet who is to come into the world!" (John 6:14). After Jesus spoke about the coming Holy Spirit, we read "When they heard these words, some of the people said, 'This really is the Prophet'" (John 7:40). Jesus' fulfillment of the Great Prophet became sharper as I proceeded through the New Testament. I eventually concluded that the Jewish followers of Yeshua and the New Testament authors believed Jesus was the prophet spoken of by Moses.

Despite the evidence from the Jewish Scriptures and the New Testament, I was curious how the rabbis viewed this Torah passage in Deuteronomy. Some rabbinical voices were adamant that there will be no prophet greater than Moses. Other rabbinical sources were closer to the idea that the Messiah will be greater than Moses.

During the time of the medieval Jewish philosopher and scholar Maimonides (AD 1135–1204), there was someone who claimed to be the Messiah. Maimonides denounced this messianic pretender in a letter he wrote to the community which was deluded by this charlatan. Maimonides wrote, "The Messiah will be a very great Prophet, greater than all the prophets with the exception of Moses our Teacher . . . His status will be higher than that of the prophets and more honorable, Moses alone excepted. The Creator, blessed be He, will single him out with features wherewith He had not singled out Moses" (Abraham Cohen, *The Teachings of Maimonides*, 1968, 121).

I was deeply struck by the letter penned by the revered Maimonides (aka Rambam). His corrective about the messianic pretender demonstrated to my inquiring mind the belief of this rabbi concerning Deuteronomy 18 and the great prophet. According to Maimonides:

- the Messiah is to be a giant cut above all the Hebrew prophets.
- the Messiah is given attributes that even Moses is lacking.

After discovering Maimonides' perspective on Deut 18, I was convinced the Messiah is to be a prophet *like* Moses but He is also a prophet *unlike* Moses. In fact, the prophet is *greater* than Moses.

The Deuteronomy 18 prophecy alone did not convince me of the Messiahship of Jesus. However, this passage from the Torah provoked me to seek out the Great Prophet. When Jesus arrived on the scene, He fulfilled every aspect of the Great Prophet by His miracles, His words, His authority and His wholehearted desire to glorify God in His teachings. Like Moses who redeemed His people from the evil of Egypt, Yeshua freed His people and the nations—not from political oppression—but from the evil of sin and provided forgiveness and eternal redemption.

If you would like to know Louis Lapides better, check out his website: www.scripturesolutions.com; and his book *Jesus or Yeshua*: *Exploring the Jewish Roots of Christianity* (Scripture Solutions, 2016).

O Lord, You have taught me the necessity of a Mediator, a Messiah, to be embraced with all my heart,
    as king to rule me,
    as prophet to guide me,
    as priest to take away my sin and death.
    And this by faith in Your beloved Son,
    who teaches me
        not to guide myself,
        not to obey myself,
        not to try to rule and conquer sin,
        but to cleave to the one who will do all for me.
In His blessed name I pray. Amen.
(Adapted from *Valley of Vision*)

Chapter 3

Messiah and Josephus

In a book about the Old Testament Messianic background of Jesus, it may seem strange to have a chapter on Josephus, the first century Jewish historian. It may appear even stranger that the following chapter is about Qumran and an obscure first century sect called the Essenes! But if we want to understand the Jewish background and context of Jesus the Messiah, it is helpful to understand what Jews in the first century were believing. So these chapters will help us understand better the Jewish world into which the Lord's Messiah emerged.

As the Bible reader moves from Malachi to Matthew, he encounters many new ideas, movements, and institutions never mentioned in the Old Testament. In the Gospels, for example, one reads about synagogues, Pharisees, Sadducees, Zealots, and Romans. These words and many others never appeared before in the Old Testament. One may also learn that the Old Testament was written in Hebrew, while the New Testament was written in Greek. He may wonder how such new ideas and changes took place. The answers to his questions lie in an understanding of what Christians call the "Intertestamental Period," while Jews generally refer to it as the "Second Temple Period." It is that very important time from approximately 400 BC to AD 1. A popular book on this period by H. A. Ironside is titled *The Four Hundred Silent Years*. However, the period was anything but "silent," since an enormous number of events took place giving birth to many movements, all of which serve as a rich background to the later events of New Testament times. The word "silent" refers to the fact that the prophetic voice was silent during this period—a fact recognized even by Jewish writers.

How can we discover what happened during these tumultuous yet fascinating years? Much of the answer to that question lies in the most thorough source for information about this period of time—the writings of the Jewish historian, Flavius Josephus.

There was a time a few hundred years ago when nearly every Christian household had, alongside the King James Bible and Pilgrim's Progress, the Whiston translation of Josephus' works. The tiny print and the crowded format of that edition, however, still deter even the most determined readers today. An excellent introduction for the modern reader is *Josephus: The Essential Works*, by Paul Maier (Kregel, 1995). In a manner that would probably please this "Jewish War Correspondent," let us answer these three questions: (1) *Who* was Flavius Josephus? (2) *What* did he write? and (3) *Why* is he important for a book on Jesus the Messiah?

Who Was Josephus?

Josephus was born around AD 37, just a few years after the death and resurrection of Jesus. He was born Joseph ben Matityahu in Hebrew, from one of the best known priestly families in Jerusalem. His mother was descended from the royal Hasmonean family, more popularly known as the "Maccabees." Josephus' own description of his childhood reveals perhaps more of his conceit than the facts.

> While still a mere boy, about fourteen years old, I won universal applause for my love of letters; insomuch that the chief priests and the leading men of the city constantly came to me for precise information on some particular in our ordinances (*Life*, page 1).

Josephus then investigated the teachings of the three main Jewish "philosophies" of his day—the Sadducees, the Essenes, and the Pharisees. He is one of the main sources on the beliefs of these important groups. At the age of eighteen, he joined the Pharisees.

After a visit to Rome, he returned to Judea at the beginning of the Jewish rebellion against the Romans. He was soon made commander of the military forces in Galilee and began to prepare for the inevitable invasion of the Roman legions. In AD 67, Josephus's forces were besieged by Vespasian's army at a Galilean fortress called Jotapata. Rather than surrender, the last ten survivors agreed to kill each other by drawing lots. But when Josephus and one other remained, he persuaded his companion that they should surrender to the Romans and hope for mercy.

Josephus soon predicted that his captor, Vespasian, would be elevated as the emperor of Rome—an event which indeed did transpire two years later. For the remainder of the war, Josephus accompanied Vespasian and later his son, Titus, until Jerusalem was conquered and burned in AD 70. Therefore, he was an eyewitness to the tragic events which transpired and has provided us with a firsthand account as an ancient Jewish war correspondent. Following the war, Josephus received Roman citizenship and took Vespasian's family name, Flavius. He was provided a villa near Rome where he spent the rest of his days writing historical, biographical, and apologetic works before dying near the end of the century.

Estimates of Josephus' character mostly center around his questionable behavior at his capture. It also should be noted that Josephus' own explanation of his actions is quite self-serving. Because he "went over" to Rome the lasting attitude of Jews toward him for centuries was one of disdain. While he always praised the deeds of his Roman patrons, he also defended the Jewish Scriptures and beliefs, and never renounced his Jewish Pharisaic faith. He blamed the Jewish rebellion on "hotheads" among them—revolutionary types who plunged a gentle, peace-loving people into the destructive caldron of a no-win war with Rome.

Whatever be the true estimation of Josephus' character, it is recognized that without his writings, our knowledge of this period would be greatly inferior. Josephus the man remains an enigma. Josephus the writer deserves our deepest appreciation.

What Did He Write?

Josephus composed four different works: one is biographical; one is apologetic; two are historical.

The Life: This is not a true autobiography but is mainly a defense of his actions at Jotapata during the war. He describes his first 25 years in two pages and devotes the rest of the space to his conduct during the early months of the rebellion against Rome. It is the least valuable of Josephus' writings.

Against Apion: Apion was an anti-Semitic Gentile who had earlier launched a slanderous attack against the Jews before the Emperor Caligula. Josephus brilliantly defends his people and their Scriptures by answering the allegations in a most interesting manner.

The Jewish War: Rightly considered as Josephus' masterpiece, this is his vivid, eyewitness account of the First Jewish Revolt against the Romans (AD 66–73). It is sometimes referred to by its Latin title *Bellum Judaicum* or "B.J." for short. Sometimes this work is published separately and is an invaluable primary source on the topography of Jerusalem. It also contains a moving description of the fortress Masada and the mass suicide/murder of the Jewish soldiers and their families.

The Antiquities: Josephus' longest work in 20 books ambitiously traces the history of the Jewish people from their Biblical roots to the beginning of the war in AD 65. His treatment of the Old Testament accounts is sometimes straightforward, almost reproducing the Biblical text word for word. However, he often adds many details, and at other times he makes glaring omissions. He includes many folklore stories found in rabbinic *midrashim*, or elaboration of the Biblical stories. For example, Josephus believed Abraham deduced that God is one through observing the celestial phenomena. According to Gen 12:10, Abraham went down to Egypt because of a famine, but according to *The Antiquities*, he went down to Egypt to debate with the wise men there. Such elaboration of the Biblical text was not viewed as "tampering" by the Jewish ancients but as examples of concentrating on the inner experience and motivation of the characters. On the other hand, he omits many episodes which he regarded as disreputable or unflattering of the Jewish "heroes," such as Jacob's trickery (Gen 27); Moses' slaying of the Egyptian (Exod 2:12); Miriam's leprosy (Num 12); and Moses' striking of the rock (Num 20:10–12). Furthermore, Rahab's embarrassing role as a prostitute was smoothed over by simply calling her an "innkeeper."

Read judiciously, *The Antiquities* provide us with a fascinating account of Jewish history including invaluable insights into such diverse characters as Alexander the Great, the Maccabees, and Herod the Great as well as some key New Testament personalities.

Bust discovered in Rome and thought to be that of Josephus

Josephus and Jesus

Many articles in our Bible dictionaries would be considerably shortened or even omitted if we did not have Josephus' writings. With all of his "faults," he remains our main historical source for the period from approximately 400 BC to AD 73. If we did not have Josephus' *Antiquities*, our Intertestamental Period courses would be almost non-existent! He also complements the New Testament accounts by providing interesting historical and cultural details which shed light on many characters and events.

Josephus discusses most of the main non-Christian characters in the New Testament such as Herod the Great (Matt 2), his son Herod Antipas (Mark 6:14–29), his grandson Herod Agrippa (cf. Acts 12), and his great grandson Agrippa II (Acts 26). He has a vivid account of Pontius Pilate's rule as well as a detailed description of the magnificent Herodian Temple in Jerusalem. As they have conducted their excavations, archaeologists have continually praised Josephus' accurate description of first-century Jerusalem. He also provides an interesting description of John the Baptist's preaching. It is Josephus who informs us that Herodias' daughter, who danced for Herod Antipas, was named Salome and that John was imprisoned in the fortress Machaerus on the eastern shore of the Dead Sea where he was also executed.

The New Testament mentions that Jesus' brother James was the leader of the church in Jerusalem (Acts 15:3–23). Josephus further describes the stoning execution of James under the instigation of the high priest Ananus in AD 62, adding the note that even the non-Christian Jews objected to this atrocity committed by the Sadducees on this Godly man.

But Josephus' most celebrated and controversial passage is his brief description of Jesus found in *The Antiquities* 18.63. The passage reads as follows:

> About this time lived Jesus, a wise man, if indeed one ought to call him a man. For he was the achiever of extraordinary deeds and was a teacher of those who accept the truth gladly. He won over many Jews and many of the Greeks. He was the Messiah. When he was indicted by the principal men among us and Pilate condemned him to be crucified, those who had

come to love him originally did not cease to do so; for he appeared to them on the third day restored to life, as the prophets of the Deity had foretold these and countless marvelous things about him. And the tribe of Christians, so named after him, has not disappeared to this day.

Sometimes this passage has been cited as evidence that Josephus was really a Jewish believer in Jesus as Messiah. However, he gives no evidence of such a belief in any of the rest of his writings, particularly in his apologetic work, *Against Apion*. While there are some critics who believe that the entire passage was inserted by a later Christian editor, the language reflects a non-Christian author (e.g., calling Jesus a "wise man" and referring to Christians as a "tribe"). There is much evidence for viewing the passage as an authentic witness to Jesus' life, death, and resurrection. It is difficult to comprehend, however, how Josephus could write the sentence that appears to be a clear confession of faith, "He was the Messiah." Perhaps the best approach is that the passage was genuinely written by Josephus with a few slight alterations by a later Christian editor. The discovery in the 1970s and subsequent publication of a 10th-century Arabic version of the *Testimonium* lacks distinct Christian terminology while sharing the essential elements of the passage. This is evidence that indicates that the Greek passage in Josephus was subject to interpolation. This approach would satisfy what appears to be both Christian and non-Christian elements in the passage. It should not be forgotten that it was Christian and not Jewish scribes who preserved the writings of Josephus! The Josephus reference thus serves as a historical attestation to Jesus' existence and to the basic form of His teaching.

We have seen that Josephus is *not* a reliable guide when he expands on the Old Testament stories for his own purposes. Also, when he writes about his own personal role in certain events, we need to read him very critically. He is indispensable, however, for a fuller understanding of the New Testament era. Read with care, he is an invaluable companion to the study of the Scriptures, especially the Gospels and Acts. Finally, his reference to Jesus, even in its original abbreviated form, is a strong argument against foolish ideas sometimes offered that Jesus never existed. The Josephus passage, written by a non-Christian, as are the other mentions of Jesus by Roman writers, puts the lie to such foolish ideas.

A helpful book that places Jesus within the Jewish world of the first century is *Jesus and His World: The Archaeological Evidence* by Craig Evans (John Knox Press, 2012).

O Lord God, may those who study history come to see that all the many facts and events and abundant stories all form part of "His Story." May they follow our Teacher and Leader and Truth, the Lord Messiah. Amen.

Chapter 4

Messiah and the Men of Qumran

Discovery of the Scrolls

Juma was beginning to get nervous since some of his goats were climbing too high up the cliffs, so he decided to climb the cliff himself to bring them back. Little did he realize on that January day in 1947 that those straying goats would involve him in what William F. Albright would call "the greatest archaeological discovery in the twentieth century." Such thoughts were far from his mind when he saw two small openings to one of the thousands of caves that dot those barren cliffs on the northwestern shore of the Dead Sea. When he tossed a rock into one of the openings, the unexpected cracking sound surprised him. What else could be in those remote caves but treasure? He called to his cousins, Khalil and Muhammad, but it was getting late, and the goats had to be gathered. Tomorrow they would return—perhaps their days of following the goats would come to an end once the treasure was uncovered!

The youngest of the three, Muhammad, rose the next day before his two "fellow treasure-seekers" and made his way to the cave. The cave floor was covered with debris, including broken pottery, but along the wall stood a number of narrow jars, some with their bowl-shaped covers still in place. Frantically Muhammad began to explore the inside of each jar, but no treasure of gold was to be found—only a few bundles wrapped in cloth and greenish with age. Returning to his cousin, he related the sad news—no treasure. No treasure indeed! The scrolls those Bedouin boys removed from that dark cave that day and in the days following would come to be recognized as the greatest manuscript treasure ever found—the first seven manuscripts of the Dead Sea Scrolls!

This was the discovery of a group of manuscripts that were a thousand years older than the oldest known Hebrew Biblical texts of that time, and they were written more than 100 years before the birth of Jesus. These manuscripts would excite the archaeological world and provide a team of translators with a gigantic task that only in the last decades has been completed.

The story of how those scrolls traveled from the hands of young Bedouin shepherds to be under the scrutinous eyes of international scholars is stranger than fiction. The above account is the accepted version of the scrolls' discovery. In recent years, however, there is scholarly skepticism about this tale, asserting that it was concocted by the Bedouin who had been illegally "excavating" for years and wanted to cover their "discovery" with this tale of accidental, unintentional good fortune! Although the details of the original "discovery" will probably never be known for sure, this much is clear. After hanging from a pole in a Bedouin tent, the seven scrolls were sold to two separate Arab antiquities dealers in Bethlehem—one was the cobbler, "Kando" who eventually became a rich man trading in antiquities such as these. From there, four were sold (for a small amount) to Athanasius Samuel, Syrian Orthodox Metropolitan at St. Mark's Monastery in the Old City of Jerusalem—the head of Kando's church.

Scholars at the American School of Oriental Research in Jerusalem who examined them were the first to realize their antiquity. John Trever photographed them and Albright soon announced that the scrolls dated from between 200 BC and AD 100. The initial announcements were then made that the oldest manuscripts ever discovered had been found in the Judean desert!

Three of the other original scrolls found by the Bedouin were sold to E. L. Sukenik, archaeologist at the Hebrew University and father of the famous Yigael Yadin. The seven scrolls finally came together at the Hebrew University under a strange set of circumstances. After touring the United States with his four scrolls and not being able to find an interested buyer, Metropolitan Samuel placed an ad in the Wall Street Journal. Yigael Yadin happened to be lecturing in New York when he saw the advertisement. Through an intermediary, the Biblical scholar Harry Orlinsky, he was able to purchase for the State of Israel these priceless scrolls for around $250,000. In February of 1955, the Prime Minister of Israel announced that the State of Israel had purchased all seven scrolls, and they were to be housed in a special museum at the Hebrew University named the Shrine of the Book, where they can still be seen today.

The initial announcement about the scrolls prompted feverish searches in the area of the original discoveries. An official archaeological expedition was begun in 1949 which eventually resulted in the discovery of ten additional caves in the surrounding area also containing scrolls. The archaeologists also directed their attention to a small ruin nearby called "Khirbet Qumran." After six seasons of intensive excavation, the scholars were sure beyond any reasonable doubt that the scrolls were copied in this community which flourished between 125 BC and AD 68.

The ruins of Qumran reveal that a substantial group of Jewish ascetics inhabited this community. Storehouses, aqueducts, ritual baths and an assembly hall were all uncovered. One of the most interesting rooms uncovered was a sort of scriptorium, identified by two inkwells discovered there along with some benches for scribes. It was in this room that many of the discovered manuscripts were probably copied. The photo in the chapter indicates the barren and isolated area to which the "men of Qumran" retired.

Description of the Scrolls

As soon as the announcement of the scrolls' discovery was made, the scholarly debates about their origin and significance began. The debates increased when the amazing contents of the scrolls were successively revealed. The seven original scrolls, from what came to be called "Cave One," comprised the following: (1) a well preserved copy of the entire prophecy of Isaiah—the oldest copy of an Old Testament book ever to be discovered; (2) another fragmentary scroll of Isaiah; (3) a commentary on the first two chapters of Habakkuk, explaining the book allegorically in terms of the Qumran brotherhood; (4) the "Manual of Discipline" or "Community Rule"—the most important source of information about the religious sect at Qumran, describing the requirements for those aspiring to join the brotherhood and how they were to behave and worship; (5) the "Thanksgiving Hymns," a collection of devotional "psalms" of thanksgiving and praise to God; (6) an Aramaic paraphrase of the Book of Genesis; and (7) the "Rule of War" which dealt with the battle between the "Sons of Light" (the men of Qumran) and the "Sons of Darkness" (the Romans?) yet to take place in the "last days," which were about to arrive.

Over eight hundred scrolls have been discovered in the 11 caves around Qumran, including fragments of every Biblical book except Esther, as well as many other non-Biblical texts. One of the most fascinating was a copper scroll which had to be cut in strips to be opened. It contains a list of 60 treasures located in various parts of Judea (none of which have been found)! Another scroll, which Israeli soldiers recovered in 1967 underneath Kando's floor, describes in detail the community's view of an elaborate Temple ritual, and has been appropriately called the "Temple Scroll."

The contents of the Dead Sea Scrolls indicate that their authors were a group of priests and laymen pursuing a communal life of strict dedication to God. Their leader was called "the Righteous Teacher" and they viewed themselves as the only true elect of Israel—they alone were faithful to the Law. They opposed the "Wicked Priest," i.e., the Jewish High Priest in Jerusalem who represented the establishment and who had persecuted them in some way. This wicked priest was probably one of the Maccabean rulers who had assumed the high priesthood between 160–140 BC. As soon as the announcement of the scrolls' discovery was made, the scholarly community began to speculate about the identity of the authors. Most scholars have identified the Qumran brotherhood with the Essenes, a Jewish sect of the Intertestamental Period described in detail by Josephus and Philo.

Whoever the men of Qumran were, their writings provide us with a background snapshot of the religious world into which Jesus came. Some have sought to draw parallels between figures in the scrolls and John the Baptist or Jesus, but an examination of such parallels reveals that the differences with these Biblical figures are greater than the similarities. Any contact of Jesus with Qumran is entirely speculative and most improbable. The suggestion that John the Baptist may have spent some time with the Qumran community is perhaps more possible since the Gospels tell us that he spent considerable time in the wilderness, the area where the Qumran community is located (Matt 3:1–3; Mark 1:4; Luke 1:80; 3:2–3). John's message, however, differed markedly from that of the Qumran brotherhood.

The most important contribution of the Dead Sea Scrolls is the cache of Biblical manuscripts that have been discovered. Up until those discoveries at Qumran, the oldest manuscripts of the Hebrew Scriptures were copies in the 9th and 10th centuries AD by a group of Jewish scribes called the Masoretes. Now we have manuscript copies of Biblical books around a thousand years older than those. These manuscripts differ in only a few details! Here is a strong illustration of the tender care which the Jewish scribes down through the centuries took in an effort to accurately copy the sacred Scriptures. On the basis of the evidence from the Dead Sea Scrolls, we can have renewed confidence that our Old Testament Scriptures faithfully represent the words given to Moses and the prophets.

Controversy of the Scrolls

In the late 1980s, a public controversy arose that had quietly raged for years in the scholarly community over the delayed publication of many scrolls. These unpublished scrolls were mainly the hundreds of scrolls found in Cave Four, which apparently was the main library of the sect. Because of the thousands of fragments in which these scrolls were found, it took a long time to piece them all together. Then the committee that had the responsibility of publishing translations of these scrolls was extremely slow in doing just that. While rumors and charges abounded of a conspiracy to keep suppressed some things discovered in the scrolls, all such charges appear now to have been greatly exaggerated.

Finally, in 1991 the logjam was broken when the Huntingdon Library in San Marino, CA, announced that any qualified scholar could examine the photographs of all the Cave Four Scrolls which they had in their possession. Since that day, the Scrolls have been available to all scholars and translations of all the scrolls have appeared so all can read them in modern languages today. Nothing damaging to the Christian or Jewish faiths was found when all the scrolls were published, despite a lot of such "hype" that sold many books and magazines.

Another great value of the scrolls is in their providing an insight into a Jewish sect that was active during the two hundred years that overlapped the beginning of the Christian era. The scrolls are invaluable for helping to establish the text of the ancient Hebrew Bible. Generally, they also provide rich background information about the world into which Jesus came.

The Judean Wilderness near Qumran; the Essenes thought that they were Isaiah's "voice crying in the wilderness"

Three Messiahs of the Scrolls

The men of Qumran fervently believed in the "last days." They had fled to the desert and were readying themselves for the coming judgment when their enemies would be vanquished when they would be given final victory according to the predictions of the prophets. The messianic hope also loomed large in the thought of the brotherhood. The evidence shows that they actually believed in three messiahs—one a prophet, the second a priest, and the third a king or prince. In the document called the *Manual of Discipline* or the *Rule of the Community,* it is laid down that the faithful should continue to live under the rule "until the coming of a *prophet* and the *anointed ones* (messiahs) of Aaron and Israel" (column 9, line 11). These three figures would usher in the age for which the community was making preparation.

In another document in Cave Four, a number of Old Testament passages are brought together which formed the basis for the messianic expectations. The first is the citation from Deut 18:18–19 where God says to Moses: "I will raise up for them a prophet like you from among their brothers." Next comes a quotation from Num 24:15–17, where Balaam foresees the rise of a *princely* conqueror: "a scepter shall rise out of Israel; it shall crush the forehead of Moab and break down all the sons of Sheth," etc. The third passage is the blessing pronounced by Moses upon the tribe of Levi (the priestly tribe) in Deut 33:8–11. The way in which these three quotations are brought together suggests that the writer(s) looked forward to the advent of a great prophet, a great prince, and a great priest.

As we have seen, three individuals in the Old Testament writings were referred to as "my anointed ones"—the prophet, the priest, and the king (Exod 29:29; 1 Sam 16:13, 24:6, 1 Kgs 19:16, Ps 105:15). Each of these was consecrated to his work by anointing with oil. The Hebrew word for "anointed" is *mashiach,* from which we get the English word *messiah.*

As we have also seen, the New Testament doctrine of the Messiah is that each of these three offices found fulfillment in the person and work of Jesus of Nazareth! The people were amazed at His feeding of the multitude and said, "This is indeed the Prophet who is to come into the world!" (John 6:14; see also John 7:40; Acts 3:22; 7:37). Jesus also was a *priest*, not from the order of Levi but from the order of Melchizedek (Ps 110:4; Heb 7), who offered Himself as a sacrifice and appears for us in the presence of His Father (Heb 9:24–26; 10:11–12). Jesus was also announced as the one who will receive "the throne of His father David, and He will reign over the house of Jacob forever, and there will be no end of His kingdom" (Luke 1:32–33). Thus, He will be acclaimed "King of Kings and Lord of Lords" (Rev 19:16).

We have found an interesting point of contact between Qumran and Christianity—a point of contact which is also a point of cleavage. The Qumran community and the early Christians agreed that in the days of the fulfillment of Old Testament prophecies there would arise a great prophet, a great priest, and a great king. These three figures remained distinct in Qumran expectation whereas the New Testament saw them unified in the person of Jesus of Nazareth.

Another Qumran manuscript provides a fascinating background to the New Testament messianic hope. It has been reconstructed from twelve small fragments, furnishing less than two columns of writing; but this much can be ascertained. It is a prediction of the birth of a *Wonderful Child*, possibly drawing on Isa 9:6–7, "For to us a child is born, to us a son is given; and the government shall be upon his shoulder, and his name shall be called Wonderful Counselor, Mighty God, Everlasting Father, Prince of Peace." According to the scroll, this child will bear special marks on His body and will be distinguished by wisdom and intelligence. He will be able to probe the secrets of all living creatures, and He will inaugurate the new age for which the faithful fervently awaited.

Soon after this manuscript was originally written, a child was born who fulfilled the hopes of Israel and inaugurated a new age!

Although the men of Qumran were mistaken in the details of their messiahs, they did expect one whose general characteristics were strikingly illustrated by Jesus of Nazareth, the Son of God and Messiah. It is not known if some early Christian brought the message of Jesus to this wilderness community. We are left only to speculate on how they would have responded to the Wonderful Child born in Bethlehem who was the Prophet, Priest, and King of Israel announced by the Hebrew prophets.

In subsequent years to these initial discoveries, one scholar believed he had found a scrap of the Gospel of Mark in the Qumran material, but there is reason to doubt that claim. Others have found references to a suffering "Messiah" and to the "Son of God" in individual scrolls. If these claims are true, there are some very strong implications. Perhaps the ideas of a suffering Messiah and a Messiah who would be the Son of God were held by Jews before the coming of Jesus and not invented by early Christians as some liberal opponents of Christianity claim.

Maybe someday we will learn if the Messianic hopes of the "men of Qumran" were ever realized before they fled their community, hiding their precious manuscripts in nearby caves. But even if we never know if they positively received the message of the gospel, their writings will continue to stimulate us to understand better that variegated group of people in first-century Israel who encountered the Prophet from Galilee.

▼

 A good introduction to Qumran and its literature with translations of the key scrolls is *The Dead Sea Scrolls: A New Translation* by Wise, Abegg, and Cook (Harper One, 2005).

O Prophet, Priest, and King. I know that there are many religious people even now who cannot see beyond religion to a living Savior and Lord. Open their eyes, Lord, that they may behold wonderful things in Your face. Amen.

Chapter 5

Messiah in Matthew

One of the great treasures of the literary deposit about Jesus is that we have four Gospel accounts about Him, not just one. There is some value in having one single harmony of the Gospels, and I use such a harmony when I teach a course on the Life of the Messiah. But the reason for four accounts is that each Gospel writer provides a distinctive view of the Messiah, not contradicting his colleagues, but complementing their descriptions of Jesus. In this chapter we survey how Matthew presents the Messiah, focusing on His Messianic role as "Son of David" and then on His Messianic "deeds."

Messiah as Son of David

In my earlier book, *Anticipating the Advent*, I mention briefly the unique and complementary genealogies of Matthew and Luke. The prominent repetition of Jesus' title "Messiah" (or "Christ" in most versions) in Matt 1:1, 16, 17, 18, and 2:4 together with other titles such as "son of David" (1:1, 20) and "King of the Jews" (2:2)

The oldest manuscript of Matthew: Papyrus 1 (University of Pennsylvania Museum)

underscore the fact that Matthew is not just recording an account of a historical figure but of a long-awaited deliverer of the Jewish people (and the Gentiles for that matter!). The geographical trek of the family from Judea to Egypt to Galilee in these chapters represents the scriptural hope for a new exodus from exile. "As the Messiah, Jesus is not just an earthly man raised up to the Davidic office; he is a divinely sent person commissioned to the messianic task who embodies the presence of God and executes His plan of redemption" (Bird, *Jesus is the Christ*, 67).

As we leave the nativity and early childhood of the Messiah in Matthew 1–2, we see the author amplifying this "Son of David" theme. His legal father Joseph is a "son of David" and thus Jesus is grafted into that Davidic line through him (Matt 1:20). Through the rest of his account, Matthew retains much of this Son of David material found also in Mark. Two men healed by Jesus introduce this Messianic title for the first time as a form of address to Him (9:27–31). Matthew records that even a Gentile "woman of Canaan" appeals to Him for her demon-possessed daughter as "Lord, Son of David" (15:22). Although He initially rebuffs her requests because His mission is focused on "the lost sheep of the house of Israel," He is impressed by her humble reply and grants her request. "Matthew here wants to press the irony that it is a Gentile woman of all people, who confesses Jesus as Lord and messianic king, and this is in contrast to his rejection within Israel" (Bird, *Jesus is the Christ*, 68). The healing of the blind men at Jericho includes this address (Matt 20:30–34; Mark 10:42–46). Jesus later presents to the Pharisees a riddle about the Messiah as the Son of David (Matt 22:42–36; Mark 12:35–37). Matthew thus affirms with the Old Testament prophets that there is a place for Gentiles in the divine plan (Amos 9:11–12; Isa 49:6; see also Paul in Acts 13:47). As Jesus began the Passion Week with His "triumphal entry," Matthew adds to the repetition of Psalm 118, "Blessed is he who comes in the name of the Lord," the acclamation "Hosanna to the Son of David" (21:9). The little children even add their Son of David acclamation (21:15). To the common people who heard him gladly (Mark 12:37), Jesus was not just any Jewish king; He was the expected Messiah and coming one foretold by the ancient prophets.

An often-overlooked aspect of these Matthean "Son of David" references is that the acclamations are often on the lips of Jewish and Gentile people of lowly social or physical status—the blind or Gentiles or the children. It appears that this is in marked contrast with the often-expressed arrogance of Israel's religious leaders who largely rejected Him. The perceptive reader will note that a prominent feature of Matthew's Messiah is His healing of the sick and freeing of the vulnerable (9:27–31; 12:22–24; 15:21–28; 20:29–34; 21:15–16). It may be initially hard to recognize that Messiah was to be a healing figure, since His roles as king and warrior and deliverer were very important to ancient Jews. Another explanation is that healings are rooted in the promise that Yahweh heals, especially in the aftermath of the exile (e.g., Exod 15:26; Deut 32:39; Jer 33:6; Hos 7:1). Note also the promises from Isaiah of a future age of healing and restoration (Isa 35:5–6). This last text was used by Jesus in response to the questions of John the Baptist in Matt 11:5. In support of this Isaianic healing thesis, Matthew quoted Isaiah in connection with Jesus' healing ministry: "In order to fulfill what was spoken through Isaiah the prophet, saying, "He Himself took our infirmities and carried away our diseases" (Matt 8:17).

"For Matthew, the Son of David is defined by mercy rather than by massacres. He comes for compassion, not combat" (Bird, *Jesus is the Christ*, 69). In this regard, the closest title to Matthew's "Son of David" is the unlikely title "Shepherd" which is mentioned as much if not more than the title "Messiah" (2:6; 9:36; 10:6, 16; 15:24; 18:12–14; 25:31–46; 26:31). When this is recognized, our minds ought to go back to David as the shepherd-king (2 Sam 5:2; Ps 78:70–72) and to Micah's promise of a ruler coming from Bethlehem who would shepherd God's people (5:1–4 and its use in Matt 2:6). To Matthew, Jesus is the Davidic Shepherd who leads the lost sheep of Israel in a new exodus marked by forgiveness, healing, and restoration.

The "Works" of the Messiah

Reference has been made above to John the Baptist's inquiry about Jesus' identity recorded in Matt 11:2–3: "Now when John in prison heard of the works of Christ, he sent *word* by his disciples and said to Him, 'Are You the One who is to come, or shall we look for someone else?'" The reference to "the works (or deeds) of Christ (Messiah)" is unique to Matthew. This verse is the first time that *Christos* has occurred in Matthew since the response of the leaders to the question of the Magi in 2:4. John had baptized Jesus as the one who fulfilled the "Messianic" promises of salvation (3:14–17). But Jesus had not destroyed Herod or the other enemies of God, as was widely expected in Jewish belief about the coming Messiah. It is not that John has lost all trust in Jesus, but the question reflects simple uncertainty about how all this was turning out. The expression "the One who is to come" or simply "the Coming One" was current terminology for the Messiah rooted in such Old Testament texts as Ps 118:26; Dan 7:13–14; Hab 2:3; and Mal 3:1. Later New Testament texts that utilize this messianic title are Acts 19:4; Heb 10:37, and Rev 1:4, 8. Even John himself had earlier utilized a form of the expression in Matt 3:11b: "He who is coming after me is mightier than I, and I am not fit to remove His sandals; He will baptize you with the Holy Spirit and fire."

While John the Baptist referred to the person of Messiah and not His "works," Jesus points to His own miracles as confirmation of His person. His response was clear and graphic: "Go and report to John what you hear and see: *the* blind receive sight and *the* lame walk, *the* lepers are cleansed and *the* deaf hear, *the* dead are raised up, and *the* poor have the gospel preached to them. And blessed is he who does not take offense at Me" (Matt 11:4b–6). He calls attention to the signs of the Messianic age (cf. Isa 35:5–6). John and his disciples can then infer that since the "works of the Messiah" are being performed, Jesus is that Messiah! John's imprisonment may not appear to him like the Messianic age of liberation, but we should try to put ourselves in his own sandals if we think harshly about his uncertainty! His imprisonment can also recall the harsh imprisonment of another Messianic prophet, Jeremiah, who suffered through his own uncertainties (see Jer 20). The "works" taking place outside his prison are indicators that the Messianic salvation has arrived, even if the Messianic judgements are yet in the future.

A later chapter in this book will explore the significance of the "Metamorphosis of the Messiah" that took place on a high mountain (Matthew 17). Immediately prior to that great event was Peter's confession of Jesus as the Messiah. Matthew 16:13-23 is another vital stage in the developments of what could also be called "Matthew's Messiology" (or more familiarly his "Christology"). This confession by Peter came at the end of Jesus' fourth withdrawal with His disciples to predominantly Gentile areas that concluded what we call His "Great Galilean Ministry." It is as clear an acknowledgement of Jesus' messiahship as could be made. Peter declares the best alternative to the answers being given to the question about what people are saying about Jesus. "You are the Christ (Messiah), the Son of the living God" (16:16). Peter, through Matthew, links the two Old Testament Messianic themes of messiahship and sonship. In the background of this graphic scene are the shrines to the god Pan. The Greek name for the area before it was renamed for another of Herod's sons was actually "Paneas." The Messianic Son of the living God points to one who is far more than a human figure. In His person, Peter has met the presence and the power of the One true God who lives and thus is not dead like the surrounding Greek gods.

Jesus blesses Peter for this correct answer, but then reminds him that his insight comes from above, not from any human authority. This is followed up with a pun and a promise that He will build His church upon this rock by playing with the similar sound and meaning of Peter's name (i.e., rock). In a sense, Peter was a foundation stone of the human edifice called the church (see Acts 1–12), but this falls far short of the Roman Catholic idea that he was the first pope who passed his office and power to succeeding generations of Roman bishops! Do not forget that the star of this drama is not Peter, but the Messiah who immediately says for the first clear time that He would suffer death as the path through which He will fulfill that Messianic role (16:21)! To this the first so-called "pope" begins to argue with Jesus against such an idea (16:22). At this point Jesus rebukes Peter for trying to stand in the way of what had to be the earthly destiny of the Messiah. It is predestined that He suffer, and if Peter tries to stand in the way of that fate, he is acting as the Old Testament Satan did, to "oppose" the plan of God that Messiah must first suffer and then enter into His glory. How ironic it is that this same Peter would later use these very expressions in describing how the Old Testament prophets described the coming Messiah: suffering then glory (1 Pet 1:11).

The role of Jesus as the Suffering Servant, in fulfillment of such Old Testament prophetic passages as Isaiah 53 and Psalm 22, will become clear during that painful but necessary period that we call the Passion Week. I have dedicated an entire volume to that time of intensive Messianic fulfillment (*Passionate about the Passion Week*).

"The Matthean portrait of Jesus is hardly monochrome" (Bird, *Jesus is the Christ*, 78). Jesus is depicted by such roles as the Son of David, the new Moses, the eschatological prophet, both Son of God and Son of Man, as well as the Suffering Servant—unbelievably diverse roles that could only be combined in the one effable person that we call "Matthew's Messiah." In summary, Jesus is the Davidic Messiah who was sent not only for the salvation of the chosen people, Israel, but also for the cleansing of those "unclean" Gentiles as well! Matthew's vision of this "coming One" moves the emphasis away from a nationalistic warrior to a different focus—a Shepherd King who brings both physical and spiritual healing to everyone, both Jew and Gentile alike. This is the eschatological healing needed by all people burdened under the illness that strikes everyone, the sickness of sin and its spiritual symptoms.

An excellent resource that influenced my writing in this chapter is *Jesus is the Christ: The Messianic Testimony of the Gospels* by Michael Bird (IVP Academic, 2012).

O God, we are sinners in Your sight; You have judged us so, and if we deny it we make You a liar. Yet in the Messiah You are reconciled to Your rebellious subjects; give us the ear of faith to hear Him, the eye of faith to see Him, the hand of faith to receive Him, the appetite of faith to feed upon Him; that we might find in Him light, riches, honor, eternal life.

(Adapted from *The Valley of Vision*)

Chapter 6

Messiah and Moses

In the previous chapter, we mentioned that Matthew was quite intentional in his effort to present Jesus the Messiah as in some way a New Moses. In this chapter, that theme will be developed and will be seen as something more than just a novel hermeneutical idea. Following Jesus' genealogy, there begin to emerge some recognizable parallels between Jesus' early life and the early years of Moses. But first we must see the overall structure of the nativity narrative in Matthew's purpose.

How the New Testament authors used the Old Testament in arguing for the Messiahship of Jesus is a fascinating subject. Let us be honest. Sometimes the New Testament authors appear to violate one of the most basic rules of hermeneutics, namely, that we should always understand a passage in its original context. Some writers have accused Matthew of doing just that in chapter 2 of his Gospel. Let's look at those "problematic" quotations and see what Matthew is actually doing with them.

Four times in Matthew 2, the author cites Old Testament texts to show how events in the young life of Jesus were foretold by the

Old Testament writers. The first quotation is in Matt 2:5–6 where the religious leaders respond to Herod's inquiry as to where the Messiah would be born. Of course Herod is actually responding to the same question posed to him by the Magi (he had no idea about the Biblical source). The scribes responded that it was in Bethlehem because the prophet said in Micah 5:2:

> And you, Bethlehem, land of Judah,
> Are by no means least among the leaders of Judah;
> For out of you shall come forth a Leader
> Who will shepherd My people Israel.

Later when the family fled to Egypt, Matthew tells us that "he remained there until the death of Herod, in order that what had been spoken by the Lord through the prophet (Hos 11:1) would be fulfilled, saying, "Out of Egypt I called My Son" (2:15).

After recording the massacre of the boys commanded by Herod, Matthew adds: "Then what had been spoken through Jeremiah the prophet (31:15) was fulfilled, saying,

> A voice was heard in Ramah,
> Weeping and great mourning,
> Rachel weeping for her children;
> And she was refusing to be comforted,
> Because they were no more (2:18).

Finally, when the family returns from Egypt and avoids going back to Bethlehem, Matthew adds that they "came and lived in a city called Nazareth, so that what was spoken through the prophets would be fulfilled: 'He shall be called a Nazarene'" (2:23).

Upon initial examination, these four incidents and textual quotations may seem to be "stretching" the idea of an Old Testament text being "fulfilled." Indeed some think that Matthew simply allegorizes these texts and throws interpretive caution to the wind. Closer examination, however, can actually lead the reader to conclude that these four examples offer the four ways in which a New Testament author cites and interprets an Old Testament text. First, Matthew's citation of Micah 5:2 is an example of a *literal* interpretation of an Old Testament text. In other words, Micah said it would be Bethlehem and it was literally fulfilled by His birth in that town. On the other hand, Matthew's use of Hos 11:1 is an example of a *typical* fulfillment of an Old Testament prophecy. Israel was often referred to as the Lord's "son" and Jesus fulfilled that role by also being God's "son." The quotation from Jer 3:15 is an example of the *analogical* fulfillment of an Old Testament text. Rachel died near Bethlehem, and just as Jewish women represented by Rachel wept at the exile and deaths of their sons in the Old Testament, so Jewish women wept at the death of their sons in Bethlehem. The final Old Testament text is not capitalized in the LSB because it is *not* an actual quotation. As a matter of fact, that "quotation" is not found in the Old Testament. Matthew is engaged in making a Messianic pun. A Nazarene was from the town of Nazareth, and the Hebrew root of that word (*netzer*) means "branch." This recalls the Messianic title in Isa 11:1: "a *branch* from his roots will be bear fruit." This title actually appears in other Old Testament texts as well (Zech 6:13). Matthew is careful to say that it was expressed not in one prophet but "through the **prophets**." In other words, this is a *summary* fulfillment of Isa 11:1 and other Old Testament texts. If I may be allowed my own pun, Jesus could therefore be called "Branch Man from Branch Town"!

About this time, some readers may feel their head spinning, but I urge you to stick with me, because there are even more exciting things to discover about how Matthew applied the Old Testament to Jesus' life and ministry. In his Gospel, Matthew creatively portrays Jesus as a new Moses. Jesus is portrayed as performing a role similar to the great mediator of Israel's Torah. This theme emerges in interesting ways even at the beginning of his narrative, although those ways can be easily overlooked. For example, when Joseph is told to return with the family from Egypt, the angel says: "for those who sought the Child's life are dead" (Matt 2:20). The words in this command are the same as the words of the Angel to Moses in Exod 2:19: "for all who were seeking your life are dead" (LXX). Like Moses was pursued by Egypt's ruler, Jesus is pursued by a hostile ruler, and that ruler slaughters children to avoid any perceived threat to his power (Matt 1:16–18). Moses fled for his life to Midian and then returned to Egypt to set free his people. Remarkably, we also see Jesus flee with his parents for His life to Egypt and then return to the Promised Land (2:13–15, 19–23). As was already mentioned, Matthew makes the connection with Moses here by quoting Hos 11:1: "Out of Egypt I have called my son." The "son" of whom Hosea references is of course the nation of Israel, liberated by Yahweh from her Egyptian slavery through the brave deeds of Moses. Although still a child when He returns to the Promised Land, Matthew portrays Jesus, like Moses, returning from His exile and beginning the work of setting God's people free.

These parallels between Jesus and Moses in chapter 2 continue the Exodus imagery with a quotation from Isaiah 40 depicting Jesus' ministry as a new Exodus (3:3). The crossing of the waters of the Red Sea where His people entered the promised land is recalled at the Jordan river by re-enacting the Red Sea parting (Josh 3). Here Jesus passes through water in His baptism (3:13–17) and is identified as God's Son (3:17), a term often applied to Israel (Exod 4:22–23). Just as Israel followed Moses into the Sinai wilderness, Jesus after passing through the waters of His baptism is then led into the desert wilderness (Matt 4:1). As under Moses the people were tested in that wilderness (Exod 15:22–27; 16:1–36), so Jesus faced His own testing at the hands of the devil (4:1–11). His quotations from Deuteronomy also recall in those chapters the nearly forty years of wandering as Moses and Israel learned to live not only on bread but on Yahweh's word (Deuteronomy 6–8).

The connections between Jesus and Moses continue when a mountain named Sinai is recalled. Jesus, like Moses, received a Torah on a mount and delivered it to his people (Exod 19ff.). One of the first acts mentioned by Matthew is that Jesus went up a mountain to deliver there His special teaching that provides a correct understanding of that original Torah (Matt 5–7), what we call the "Sermon on the Mount." Matthew portrays this "New Moses" as repeating the Sinai event at the outset of His career. He launches that sermon by declaring: "Do not think that I came to abolish the Law or the Prophets; I did not come to abolish but to fulfill" (Matt 5:17). As the New Moses, He is not delivering an entirely new law. He causes Israel to hear the same Torah delivered by the first Moses, but given a true interpretation by the Second Moses.

With all of the similarities with the message delivered by the First Moses, there is still a way that Jesus on this mountain surpasses Moses on Mount Sinai. Jesus is not like the receiver of the original Torah, who broke the tablets when Israel failed so miserably (Exod 32). Jesus instead sits down on the mountain, assuming the well-recognized posture of a Rabbi-teacher (see Matt 23:2). It is Jesus who authoritatively delivers this law, taking the place of Yahweh himself in the Exodus account. Jesus portrays in His combination of authority and humility the very presence of the One who is both Israel's God and the Light to the people He is calling together. Unlike Moses, though, this mediator does not stand entirely on the side of the people, standing between them and their Maker. He is a new Moses, but He is also someone who is greater than Moses (see Hebrews 3–4).

Painting of Moses in the Basilica of the Transfiguration, Mount Tabor

---

For an accurate portrayal of Jesus in the manner we have sought to portray him in this chapter, see *The New Moses: A Matthean Typology* by Dale Allison (Wipf and Stock, 2013 reprint).

O Father, You are enthroned to hear my prayers.
O Jesus, Your hand is outstretched to receive my petitions.
O Spirit, You are willing to help my infirmities, to show me my need, to supply my words, to pray within me, to strengthen me that I not faint in my supplication. Amen.
(Adapted from *The Valley of Vision*).

Chapter 7

Messiah in the Water

Although it has taken us some time and space to get to the first "Crisis of the Christ," it is important that we try to understand the Old Testament / Jewish / Messianic context that Jesus entered in what became the first century of our era. Since we gave attention to His Advent in an earlier book, we now turn to the first significant public event in what we call "Messiah's Ministry." All are agreed that it is when He publicly entered the waters of baptism.

We know him today as "John the Baptist," but in the first century his official name would have been Yohanan ben Zechariah. The announcement of his miraculous conception and birth to the elderly couple, Zechariah and Elizabeth, is recorded in Luke 1. We learn that relatives were surprised when Elizabeth wanted to name the child what we spell today as "John." The mute Zechariah wrote on a tablet this name that was given to him by the angel. The moving chapter ends with the following statement which leads to the subject of this chapter. "And the child continued to grow and to become strong in spirit, and he lived in the desolate regions until the day of his public appearance to Israel"

(Luke 1:80). The "desolate regions" or the "desert places" are what every Israeli would call today "the wilderness."

Now fast forward to Luke 3 and Matthew 4 and Mark 1. The first event that is recorded by all three of the Synoptic Gospels is the ministry of John the Baptist and his baptism of the Messiah. Actually the Gospel of John also records these events in chapters 1–3, although from a different perspective. Because we are seeking to understand better the Jewish/Old Testament context of Jesus, it is appropriate also that we try to see John in that same context. Because his birth parents were already elderly, it is probable that John was orphaned at an early age. That fact contributes to Luke's statement that John emerged publicly from the "wilderness" region of Judah near the Dead Sea (Luke 1:80). Let me encourage the reader also to consider that John may have spent time in that Essene community of ascetics who had their settlement at a place we call "Qumran" on the northwestern shore of the Dead Sea. There are some reasons that make this more than a wild conjecture. Josephus, whom we have already studied, tells us that the Essenes at Qumran were known for adopting orphans and raising them in their sect. Their settlement was in the dry and barren wilderness, where John spent a period of his life according to Luke 3:2–3. The Essenes also were quite ascetic in their practices and culinary habits, which fits what we know about John's different appearance and diet (see Matt 3:4). From the archaeological discoveries at the Essene's settlement and from the texts discovered there, it is evident that they practiced ritual immersion on a daily basis. John also came in the wilderness baptizing (immersing) and drew crowds from all over the region to these very public events. The Essenes utilized Isaiah's reference to a voice in the wilderness (40:3) and considered themselves collectively as that very voice calling out to the rest of the people of Israel. Matthew tells us that John was individually using that same text: "For this is the one referred to by Isaiah the prophet, saying,

> The voice of one crying in the wilderness,
> 'Make ready the way of the Lord,
> Make His paths straight!'

Thus John the Baptist's ministry should be understood in both the Old Testament and the first-century context in which it emerged. At the same time, however, we need to be careful to add that if John emerged from the Essene community, he changed some of their distinctive characteristics. Their baptism was daily; John's baptism was initiatory and not repeated. Furthermore, while the Essenes saw their ministry as the fulfillment of that voice in the wilderness, the Gospel writers make it clear that John himself was that voice and not any sect, even if his voice emerged from that sect! There is one more fact about John's baptism that may not sit well with my Presbyterian friends. The mode of this baptism among the Essenes was immersion and that was John's practice as is evident from the basic meaning of the verb "baptize" and also from the fact that it was practiced in a place where there was plenty of water (John 3:23), something not needed if the practice was anything other than immersion!

Was there evident in the ancient Judaism of John's day such a practice of initiatory baptism? Yes, there was, and it is a practice still observed today among religious Jews. While orthodox women often immerse themselves in what is called a *mikveh* (after their monthly and the birth of a child), even Orthodox men will do this every Friday in preparation for the Sabbath. That is still not initiatory, but is done often. What is done once is the immersion in a *mikveh* of a Gentile man or woman who converts to Judaism. Perhaps this practice, established before the coming of John's baptism, is what angered the religious Jews who were being told to repent and be baptized. This upstart John was telling them that no matter how religious they were, they must repent and be immersed like an unclean Gentile! This explains their angry rejection of John's counsel. "Therefore bear fruit in keeping with repentance; and do not suppose that you can say to yourselves, 'We have Abraham for our father'; for I say to you that from these stones God is able to raise up children to Abraham'" (Matt 3:9). They were probably crying out, "Who is this country preacher to tell us, the religious elite of Israel, that we need to stoop to the requirement for Gentile converts?!"

That was John's ministry to the nation and the response from all levels of society is witnessed by the statement, "Then Jerusalem was going out to him, and all Judea, and all the district around the Jordan; and they were being baptized by him in the Jordan River, as they confessed their sins" (Matt 3:5–6). But one day, a young man with a Galilean accent patiently stood in line, waiting His turn for baptism. It is often forgotten that this young man was a distant cousin of John's. While we have no idea about whether these cousins ever hung out in their youth (doubtful), John eventually recognized Jesus (see John 1:31–33). He initially demurred from baptizing Him, humbly acknowledging his own need to be baptized by Jesus (Matt 3:14). Do not forget that John had already announced that his baptism was preparing for the Messiah's arrival. "As for me, I baptize you with water for repentance, but He who is coming after me is mightier than I, and I am not fit to remove His sandals; He will baptize you with the Holy Spirit and fire" (3:11). The fire he referred to is probably not the Holy Spirit (see Acts 2), but was a reference to the fiery judgment on those who refuse to repent. He had referred to this judgment by fire in the verse before and after this statement (3:10, 12).

Jesus' response to John's hesitance is insightful but also challenging as to what He meant. Jesus answered and said to him, "'Permit *it* at this time; for in this way it is fitting for us to fulfill all righteousness.' Then he permitted Him" (3:15). The reason why the Jewish Messiah wanted to be baptized is two-fold. First, it was to clearly identify Himself to John (see John 1:33–34). Second,

The traditional site of Jesus' baptism in the lower Jordan River

here He states that their act was to "fulfill all righteousness." But what does that really mean? The grammar of the passage plus an appeal to a great Messianic text provides the answer. Jesus uses the plural "us" when He says that by this act *we* will fulfill all righteousness. John and Jesus together are performing a very important deed. That act and reference to "righteousness" is found in the passages about the Suffering Servant described in Isaiah. There we read: "By His knowledge the Righteous One, My Servant, will justify the many, as He will bear their iniquities" (53:11). John's action of setting aside Jesus as the Righteous one who needed no repentance was part of their mutual unveiling so that the Righteous Messiah, so graphically revealed in Isaiah 53, will assume His role that will be so graphically fulfilled in the event of the coming "Passion Week."

As we now consider the important spiritual phenomena that accompanied Jesus' baptism, I turn to one of my favorite New Testament scholars, Richard Bauckham, to whom I am indebted for some of the thoughts in the rest of this chapter. Our focus will be on Mark's brief but full account of the baptism.

Mark's account of the baptism is the first appearance of Jesus in his Gospel. His appearance, however, is also the appearance of all three of the Divine persons: the Father, the Son, and the Spirit. If we use the term "Trinity," which became familiar in later theological language, we should remind ourselves that Mark would not recognize it. The truth of the triune God, however, emerges from an honest reading of the account. This is the beginning of what we might call the "Trinitarian story" that Mark will relate. It is true that we can find hints of the Trinity in the Old Testament, but we must be honest that the truth does not leap off the page to every reader. It was the story of Jesus as He is revealed in the Four Gospels that moved Christians from the earliest period to recognize that the one God made Himself known in such a way through His Son that an eternal relationship between them was recognized. The Spirit so evident in the Old Testament also became known as the Spirit who empowered Jesus and who was later sent by Jesus to His disciples.

Here at the public outset of Jesus' ministry the three persons make their presence known. Let us read Mark's words and think about them: "And immediately coming up out of the water, He saw the heavens opening, and the **Spirit** like a dove descending upon Him; and a **voice** came out of the heavens: "You are My beloved **Son**, in You I am well-pleased. And immediately the Spirit drove Him *to go* out into the wilderness" (1:10–12). While this account takes place on earth, the message comes from heaven. The heavens were literally "torn apart" and Jesus experienced the Spirit in the form of a dove descending on Him. The Greek verb used in 1:10 for "opening" or "split" is a surprising word to describe such a vision. One thinks of Ezekiel's vision when he saw the heavens "opened" (1:1) and the dying Stephen as he looked into heaven and saw Jesus (Acts 7:56), as well as Peter seeing in a dream a sheet lowered from heaven to earth (Acts 10:11), while John saw a door opened in heaven (Rev 4:1). The reason Mark uses such an almost violent term lies in a vision of the prophet Isaiah. Mark has already mentioned that his account is a fulfillment of Isaiah's prophecies (1:2-3). Isaiah 40 and following was one of the most important Old Testament passages for the early Christian authors. A survey of the Gospels, Acts and Paul unveils dozens of references to this so important section of Isaiah—and not only the great Suffering Servant passages of chapters 42-53 (see, e.g., Acts 13:47/Isa 49:6 and Rom 11:34/Isa 40:13).

Notice the vivid language of Isa 64:1: "O that you would tear the heavens and come down, so that the mountains would quake at your presence." With Moses and his brothers as witnesses, Yahweh came down on Mount Sinai and the mountains quaked (Exod 29:18; Ps 68:7-8; Hab 3:6, 10). Bauckham observes: "The image of tearing the heavens apart is appropriate here because it suggests an irruption of divine power into the world" (*Who is God*, 94). Therefore, when Mark employs the same language of "tearing open," he means to convey that the prophet's prayer in Isa 64:1 above is now being answered. The Lord God has again descended from heaven. His Son has now been empowered for ministry by the Divine Spirit and Yahweh is present again amongst His people. Further consideration should also be given to Mark's use of this verb (*skizo*) in the tearing of the veil in the inner sanctuary of the Temple during the crucifixion (15:38).

Bauckham asks a second question about this event. Why does Jesus see in this vision a dove? While commentators and preachers debate if this was an actual dove, certainly Jesus sees the Spirit in the form of a dove. Ancient rabbis pointed to the language of Gen 1:2b that the Spirit of God hovered over the face of the water is the expression to describe a mother dove hovering over her chicks. "Then the meaning could be that the Spirit descending onto Jesus was initiating the work of a new creation, the renewal of creation by the same divine Spirit who was active in the original creation" (Bauckham, *Who is God*, 96).

We now consider the important words uttered at this sublime event. The Father not only calls Jesus His Son, but He says: "You are my beloved Son." The Hebrews could use that special term to mean "only" son, especially loved because he or she is an only child. When Yahweh commanded Abraham to offer his son Isaac, the text is clear that Isaac is referred to as Abraham's "only son" (Gen 22:2, 12, 16). The LXX version uses that same Greek word that is in Mark, *agapetos*. Others could legitimately be called "sons of God" for various reasons (see Gen 6:2; Job 1:6; Ps 82:6), but Jesus the Messiah is singled out as God's son in a unique sense—as the Father's only son who is dear to His Father's heart. This term cannot be exhausted by a theological over-defining; it expresses the warmth and love of emotional attachment. This truth of Jesus as God's Son opens Mark's Gospel in its title (1:1; "Son of God"); closes the book at the crucifixion (15:39; "Son of God"); and is the center piece of his book at the Transfiguration (9:7, "Beloved Son").

"For Mark, as for other New Testament authors, it is the most meaningful description of Jesus" (Bauckham, *Who is God*, 98). Sonship is not just a status or an office; it expresses a deep relationship that binds together the Father and His Begotten One. While Mark from this point onward will focus on Jesus, this baptismal vision, so rooted in Old Testament terminology, prepares the reader to expect that the Spirit will continuously be at work in Jesus' ministry (see Mark 3:29) and that this One who has received publicly the Messianic anointing of the Spirit will continuously be in touch with His heavenly Father (Mark 9:7) and sustained by a Father's love while carrying out His Father's will. This relationship will ultimately be expressed in that deepest of emotional scenes by Jesus' prayer in Gethsemane of "Abba Father" (Mark 14:36).

As was mentioned above, a remarkable example of reading Mark's portrayal of Jesus in light of the Old Testament can be found in Richard Bauckham's little volume, *Who is God?* (Baker, 2020). It examines with great skill a number of texts that are what the subtitle says: *Key Moments of Biblical Revelation*. We will return to this volume when we later consider "Messiah's Metamorphosis" or Transfiguration.

 O Lord Jesus, come to me;
O Divine Spirit, rest upon me;
O Holy Father, look upon me in mercy.
For the sake of Your well-beloved. Amen.
(Adapted from *Valley of Vision*)

Chapter 8

Messiah in the Wilderness

Just as the Gospels come together (for the first time) in recording John's baptism of Jesus, the three Synoptic Gospels each record an account of Jesus' temptation in the wilderness. Although Mark's account is rather brief (1:12–13) compared to that of Matthew (4:1–11) and Luke (4:1–13), he has some unique items to add to the mix. Our approach to this series of the Messiah's experiences in the wilderness will be two-fold. First, we will look at some historical and literary features of the event to better understand what happened. Second, we will then look at the Old Testament background of the temptations and draw some broader theological and spiritual insights from this important "Crisis of the Christ." At this point we will introduce the reader to what may be a new term, the "intertextuality" of the Scriptures.

As to the locale of the temptation, the obvious word is the "wilderness" (Matt 4:1/Mark 1:12/Luke 4:1). Anyone familiar with the geography of Israel knows that this is the region of Israel immediately west of the lower Jordan and the Dead Sea. The ancient city of Jericho lies there as a sort of doorway into the land

(Joshua 2–6). The hill immediately west of Jericho is referred to traditionally as the "Mount of Temptation" and a Greek Orthodox monastery hangs precipitously there from the sheer cliff face. While we cannot be dogmatic about it being the actual site of the Temptation, it is certainly the location of a much earlier event: where the spies were told by Rahab to flee until the search party returned (Josh 2:16, 22). Another common theme in the temptation accounts is the role of the Spirit who had descended on Jesus in the Jordan River. Matthew and Luke say that the Spirit "led" Jesus to the wilderness while Mark uses a very strong verb: "And immediately the Spirit **drove** (*ekballo*) Him *to go* out into the wilderness." We will later notice the parallels with both Moses and Israel in the wilderness. The presence of the Spirit with them in the wilderness wanderings could be the background here. In Jesus' case, His empowerment with the Divine Spirit will now be tested to see if He would be able to succeed where Israel failed in their own wilderness wanderings. Mark's concise account graphically adds the stark reminder that "He was with the wild beasts ... and the angels were ministering to Him" (Mark 1:13).

Matthew and Luke record the three specific temptations, although in a different order. Matthew probably records the original order, since he uses the temporal adverb "then" to connect the three (4:1, 5, 10, 11). The word "Devil," meaning "slanderer," only appears in the New Testament in our English Bibles, but the same creature answers to the name "Satan" from the Old Testament (1 Chr 21:1; Job 1:6; Zech 3:1), where the Greek word for "Devil" appears in the Greek Septuagint. In Matthew, the Devil frames the temptations in three conditional clauses, each beginning with "if." (1) "If You are the Son of God, command that these stones become bread"; (2) "If You are the Son of God, throw Yourself down"; and (3) "If You fall down and worship me ... all these things I will give You." (I have reversed the order of the "if" and "then" parts of the conditional sentence in the third

The "Mount of Temptation" in the wilderness where Jesus was tested after His baptism

one). It is interesting that, in the Greek, the first and second "if" clauses assume the reality that Jesus *is* the Son of God, while the third one expresses it as a condition that is not assumed. In other words, the Devil says: "Since you are the Son of God, then do this." In the third one, he cannot assume that Jesus will fall down and worship him. Jesus responds to each of these temptations with a verse from Scripture, particularly from two chapters in Deuteronomy:

1. But He answered and said, "It is written, 'Man shall not live on bread alone, but on every word that proceeds out of the mouth of God'" (Matt 4:4/Deut 8:3).
2. Jesus said to him, "Again, it is written, 'You shall not put the Lord your God to the test'" (Matt 4:7/Deut 6:16).
3. Then Jesus said to him, "Go, Satan! For it is written, 'You shall worship the Lord your God, and serve Him only'" (Matt 4:10/Deut 6:13). (The LSB capitalizes the words

The possible "Pinnacle" of the Temple where Jesus was tempted

from Deuteronomy to make it easier to recognize the Old Testament quotations).

It is obvious that the general location of the temptations was the "wilderness" but the second one takes place on the pinnacle of the temple in Jerusalem, a place that could be seen by most people in Jerusalem. If Jesus had jumped from there it would have been a big show for everyone when the angels rescued Him from certain death! Medieval rabbis even taught that when the Messiah came he would stand on the roof of the Temple and proclaim to the world who he was (*Pesikta Rabbati* 36). But Jesus would not put His Father to the test by doing such a foolish act. The devil tempted Jesus, but Jesus told him not to tempt the Father! The devil had wrongly applied Ps 91:11–12 ("he will command his angels to guard you…"), so an old saying goes that "even the Devil can quote scripture" (for his own purposes).

So the Messiah passed these three tests, one might even say "with flying colors." Matthew's epilogue is eloquent: "Then the devil left Him; and behold, angels came and *began to* minister to Him" (4:11). But what does all this mean theologically and spiritually? And how does the Old Testament help us to address those important questions?

The fact that there were specifically *three* temptations has given rise to many interpretations, both Biblically and homiletically! One homiletical application is a comparison to the three-fold "lusts" or "desires" in 1 John 2:16: "For all that is in the world, the lust of the **flesh** and the lust of the **eyes** and the boastful **pride of life**, is not from the Father, but is from the world." While it is possible to see a parallel between the focus of each temptation and each "lust" in 1 John, that is more an application by John, possibly with his eye on Matthew 4. But that does not really shed light on the significance of Jesus' temptations in light of their possible Old Testament background. Another approach could be called the "Adam View" since it focuses on the threefold appeal to Adam and Eve that the fruit was good for **food**, a delight to the **eyes**, and desirable to make one **wise**" (Gen 3:6). In this view, Jesus, the second Adam, succeeds in the role in which the first Adam failed. In his excellent book, *The Last Adam* (Baker Academic, 2017), Brandon Crowe argues that the presence of "wild beasts" in the Markan temptation argues for the idea that Jesus' peaceful co-existence with the animals points to His authority over them and recalls Adam's original dominion over the animals in Eden. He also points out that the strong word for Jesus being driven out of the river and into the wilderness (*ekballo*), is also used for Adam's being driven out of Eden (Gen 3:24, in the Septuagint). His presence in the wilderness also evokes prophetic imagery of a peaceful messianic age in which animals do not attack (Isa 11:6–9; 65:25). Thus Mark's portrayal of Jesus as the last Adam marks the beginning of a new creation, which of course will still be completed in the end times (Crowe, *The Last Adam*, 24–26).

It is hard *not* to see some connection and contrast with the failure of Adam and Eve in a perfect environment with Jesus' success in an alien environment. But there may be more than an "Adam Christology" at work in these Temptation accounts. How about this connection, not with Adam, but with Moses? What was Jesus doing all those forty days in addition to fasting? Because fasting is often connected with prayer, perhaps we should consider a direct dependence of Jesus on the experience of Moses who for forty days and nights was interceding for Israel's sins. Look at Deut 9:25–26 for this possible "Moses Christology": "So I fell down before the LORD the forty days and nights, which I did because the LORD had said He would destroy you. I prayed to the LORD and said, 'O Lord GOD, do not destroy Your people, even Your inheritance, whom You have redeemed through Your greatness, whom You have brought out of Egypt with a mighty hand."

This reference to Deuteronomy also suggests that a clearer focus than an Adam or a Moses connection can be found in what could be called an "Israel Christology," because the three texts that Jesus cites in response to the Devil are *not* cited from Genesis but from Deuteronomy. And the chapters mentioned (6–8) focus on Israel's sojourn in another wilderness that was quite similar to the Judean wilderness. Yes, Adam failed in a perfect world, but Israel failed in a fallen world. Israel was often called "God's son" (Exod 4:22–23; Hos 11:1) and after their deliverance and passing through the waters of the sea (being baptized to Moses in that sea, 1 Cor 10), Israel still failed. Jesus also went through the waters as God's Son, was then severely tried, but passed the test! Notice the point that Israel was God's son. The devil tests the Messiah by calling into question precisely that identity announced for Jesus at His baptism; compare "This is my beloved Son" with the devil's "If You are the Son of God." Will His messianic calling be fulfilled by miraculous making of bread or displays of power from the Temple's heights, or will His vocation be displayed in humble obedience to His Father? It is interesting that a future reign of glory over all earthly kingdoms will be the right of the Messiah, but will He opt for that now or choose the path to that glory which will be through suffering on a cross (see 1 Pet 1:10–11)? This also adds some octane to Jesus' statement at His baptism that His calling was to fulfill all righteousness—as the Messianic Suffering Servant (Isa 53:11). Israel's King will observe God's will in His Torah (Deut 17:18–20). Jesus obeyed His Father's will here at the very outset of His Messianic ministry. It is interesting in this regard to observe that Jesus eventually did these things that the Devil asked, in one way or another, but He will not do them *now*—at the behest of the Devil and by taking a shortcut to avoid the cross that was a necessary part of His Messianic calling.

I have a concluding suggestion about the above possible connections between Jesus in the wilderness going back to Adam, or to Moses, or to Israel. Perhaps we should not be forced to decide which option is correct. If we seek to discover an intertextual thread from a New Testament text to an Old Testament text, why could that thread not also connect back through more than one source? It would still be one intertextual thread, one beautiful connection that goes back from Jesus in a Judean wilderness through Israel in the Sinai wilderness, through Moses on the mountain, and ultimately back to Adam in a garden?

There is enough theology in all of this to satisfy our theological cravings, so I will not spend much time and space on the vexing question that theologians refer to as the peccability or impeccability of the Savior during His incarnation. In laymen's terms the question is this: could Jesus have sinned in His humanity? We know that He did not sin, but passages like this and His agony at Gethsemane and the language of Hebrews 5:7–9 with Jesus somehow through His testing becoming "perfect" lead some of us to conclude that He could have sinned but did not. Such resistance to temptation actually helps us to understand better a sympathetic Messiah! We appreciate even more the help that Jesus gives us at the throne of grace because it comes from one who was tested severely but passed, and one who can provide us with the mercy and grace that will help us so we can also pass those tests (Heb 4:14–16)!

At this point some of my lay readers may be overwhelmed by so much theology surrounding what appears to be a simple series of temptations that Jesus succeeded in handling. Some may be wondering if a practical lesson can emerge from this deep and profound "drama in a desert!" I suggest that there is something very practical that we can take from Jesus' example. The question is: how did Jesus succeed in His battle against sin and how can I also succeed in my daily battle with the Tempter? My answer is to point you to how Jesus fought back against the Devil. He did not argue with the Tempter, but neither did He run from the temptation. He quoted His Heavenly Father's word as His response to the Devil's attacks. The Apostle Paul, in describing the believer's armor to wear in our struggles against the satanic powers (Eph 6:10–18), tells us to use one offensive weapon, "the sword of the Spirit, which is the word of God" (6:17). If the Son of God needed His Bible with Him to succeed, in our own battles we need our Bibles at our sides and in our hearts and in our mouths!

▼

 In addition to Brandon Crowe's book, *The Last Adam* (Baker Academic, 2017), which was mentioned in the chapter, another heavy duty but helpful work in a Messianic context is *The Messianic Theology of the New Testament* by Joshua Jipp (Eerdmans, 2020). Instead of starting with the Messianic promises and working forward, Jipp reads the New Testament accounts and then looks back to the Messianic promises to see how we should best read them in the New Testament.

 Almighty God, You called Abraham, Isaac, Jacob and the prophets; and, through Jesus Your Messiah, You called the twelve apostles. By Your grace, You have called me. But first I must be tested, even as Your Son was tested in a barren wilderness. May Your word arise in my heart and mouth as it did in His heart and mouth. Through Him I pray. Amen.

Chapter 9

Messiah in the Hometown

I was scared stiff at the prospect of preaching in my home church! A few years earlier, I had come to the Lord through the ministry of a church in Spartanburg, South Carolina. Everyone at home knew me as the kid who went off to study for the ministry. While in college during the past year I had preached on the street corners and in the jails of Asheville and Charlotte, NC. This was my first church sermon, however, and I had been asked to deliver it to my home church. The preacher boy had come home. I prepared and prayed and prayed and prepared. Finally, the big day arrived. I began my message and it seemed to be going well—too well, I soon discovered. I was picking up such speed that, to my utter dismay, fourteen minutes after I began the sermon, I had finished everything I had to say! Not being yet skilled in how to just talk to fill up the time, I finally just finished and sat down. While the pastor gave the closing prayer, I slipped off the platform, headed down a hallway, sat down on the back steps of the church, and began to cry. I thought I had failed miserably before everyone who knew me in my home church. Soon a wise elder found me and brought me back to the vestibule, where a large number of perplexed people greeted me warmly. I discovered that the people were not as upset with me as I had thought. They rather liked the idea of a fourteen minute sermon!

I think of that experience whenever I read the account in Luke 4:16–30 that describes Jesus coming home and preaching in His own synagogue. The passage begins with words pregnant with emotion: "And He came to Nazareth, where He had been brought up" (Luke 4:16a).

The Situation

"And as was His custom, He entered the synagogue on the Sabbath and stood up to read" (Luke 4:16b). In modern Nazareth, down a back alley and about six feet below the present street level, is the reconstructed ruin of an ancient synagogue. Hebrew inscriptions found in the nineteenth century on nearby columns support the 1,300-year-old tradition that this was possibly the site of the first-century synagogue Jesus attended and where He delivered His dramatic sermon toward the beginning of His public ministry. For many years, a highlight of my visits to Israel with students was gathering together in this partially reconstructed room and remembering the events Luke so graphically recounts in chapter four of his Gospel.

The passage comes alive when we recognize how it closely fits with time-honored Jewish customs and practices. In ancient times, even as it is today, the Sabbath service consisted of prayers; a reading from the first five books of Moses; a reading from one of the books of the prophets, and finally a sermon. The Scripture readings follow a definite cycle all over the world in which the entire Pentateuch (or Torah) is covered in one year. Each of these Torah readings is then supplemented by a selected reading called the *Haftarah* taken from one of the Prophets. This procedure, followed by a sermon, is not only witnessed to in this passage but is also illustrated in the journeys of Paul in Acts 13:14–15:

> But going on from Perga, they arrived at Pisidian Antioch. And on the Sabbath day, they went into the synagogue and sat down. And after the reading of the Law and the Prophets the synagogue officials sent to them, saying, "Brothers, if you have any word of exhortation for the people, say it."

According to the passage in Luke, the initial prayers and reading from the Torah had already been concluded. Those readings were done by laymen in the congregation, since there were no resident congregational rabbis at that time. As a young man who had achieved some notoriety away from home, Jesus now assumed His responsibility to be one of the readers of the *Haftarah* or the selection from the Prophets. Let us follow Luke's terse description. "And the scroll of the prophet Isaiah was handed to him." Unlike today, there were no "books" as we know them. The "codex," or book form, did not appear until the second century AD. Each individual Biblical book, except for a few small ones bound together, was in a separate scroll, rolled together when not being used. The Isaiah scroll was handed to Jesus by an attendant (see v. 20), or *chazzan*, the person in charge of the synagogue service and the scrolls.

In the synagogue liturgy, selections from Isaiah are normally read in the summer months of July and August. For many years this had been practiced in the Nazareth synagogue. Thus, we know certain things about the situation in Nazareth at that time. It was probably a hot, Saturday morning in August when Jesus read from the Prophet Isaiah. This Sabbath, however, was different from any other. What Jesus read, and how He applied this text, resulted in a near riot, the likes of which that little Jewish congregation certainly had never witnessed.

Torah Scroll and "pointer" used in the Synagogue reading

The Exposition

And He opened the scroll and found the place where it was written,

> The Spirit of the Lord is upon Me,
> Because He anointed Me to preach the gospel to the poor.
> He has sent Me to proclaim release to the captives,
> And recovery of sight to the blind,
> To set free those who are oppressed,
> To proclaim the favorable year of the Lord.

And He closed the scroll, gave it back to the attendant and sat down, and the eyes of all in the synagogue were fixed on Him. And He began to say to them, "Today this Scripture has been fulfilled in your hearing" (Luke 4:17b–21).

The passage Jesus read was Isa 61:1–2. We know that Isaiah 61 is part of the synagogue reading schedule, even until today.

Was it the assigned reading for that Sabbath or did Jesus choose this passage because it was so appropriate at this stage of His ministry? We cannot know the answer for sure, but I tend to think that Jesus simply was following the passage that was scheduled for that day and it "just so happened" to be such an appropriate passage as that found in Isaiah 61.

Jesus cut off the reading of Isa 61:2 right before the statement, "and the day of vengeance of our God," and He then stated clearly that the section He had read was being fulfilled that very day (Luke 4:21). The promise in Isaiah that the Lord would send an "anointed" one to preach the gospel, heal the brokenhearted, proclaim deliverance, and set free the oppressed was being fulfilled in His coming as the Messiah. The statement, "The Spirit of the Lord is upon me because he has anointed me," is the same as saying, "I am the Messiah." Messiah is the Hebrew word *Mashiach*, or anointed one. As you probably know well by now, the English word "Christ" is derived from the Greek translation of this Hebrew word. No clearer claim to messiahship could be made than to identify Himself as He did with the anointed one promised in Isa 61:1.

Jesus, however, did *not* fulfill another aspect of the Messiah's role that is mentioned in the passage. It is important to note not only what He did quote, but what He did not quote. He stopped His reading right before the words that conclude Isa 61:3: "the day of vengeance of our God." That is because those words describing the judgmental role of the Messiah would be fulfilled not in His first coming but at His Second Coming (Rev 19:11–16). Here is one of those indications that Jesus did not fulfill all of the Messianic prophecies of the Old Testament, but only those related to the work He accomplished in His first coming. The prophecies related to His judging the world will be fulfilled in connection with His second coming. How precise is the fulfillment of the messianic prophecies!

Another significance to Jesus' use of Isa 61:1–2 in the Nazareth synagogue concerns the phrase, "to preach the acceptable year of the Lord" (Isa 61:2; Luke 4:19, KJV). Other translations render this phrase, "the year of the Lord's favor" (ESV), or "the favorable year of the Lord" (LSB). Many commentators believe the phrase is a reference to the Year of Jubilee, which took place every 50 years (Lev 25:30). During that year, freedom was proclaimed to captives and each person was to return to his own property. What makes this even more striking is that, according to Jewish reckoning, a Jubilee year occurred during Jesus' ministry. According to the information given by the Jewish historian, Josephus, it can be calculated that a Jubilee year occurred in 26–27 AD. Jesus' quotation and application took account of the actual Jubilee year in which His ministry began and from which it gained a background of Messianic expectancy.

Historians agree that the Jewish people had ceased to observe the details of the Jubilee year during the Second Temple Period. They continued, however, to mark the years, although they did not observe the customs in the year. The revolutionary claim that Jesus was making was that He was initiating the spiritual Jubilee redemption. This must have exploded like a bombshell in the synagogue that Saturday morning in Nazareth. No doubt many wondered, "How could this young man, who grew up down the street and played with us as a child, be the promised Messiah who will set us free?" Physical bondage, as bad as it is to those who endure it, is not as permanent and grievous as spiritual bondage. It is only by faith in Him that true freedom is obtained—freedom from fear, guilt, man-made ordinances, and sin and its consequences.

The Application

Despite the urgency of Jesus' claim, it appears that the truth of all this did not immediately hit His hearers. Initially, they marveled at the young man's sermon. "And all spoke well of him and marveled at the gracious words that were coming from his mouth. And they said, 'Is not this Joseph's son?'" (Luke 4:22). However, Jesus drove home the application they needed:

> And He said to them, "No doubt you will quote this proverb to Me, 'Physician, heal yourself! Whatever we heard took place at Capernaum, do also here in your hometown as well.'" And He said, "Truly I say to you, no prophet is welcome in his hometown. But I say to you in truth, there were many widows in Israel in the days of Elijah, when the sky was shut up for three years and six months, when a great famine came over all the land, and yet Elijah was sent to none of them, but only to Zarephath, *in the land* of Sidon, to a woman who was a widow. And there were many lepers in Israel in the time of Elisha the prophet, and none of them was cleansed, but only Naaman the Syrian" (Luke 4:23–27).

Jesus knew that even when His hearers realized that they were the blind ones who needed to see and the captives who needed to be freed, they still would not readily accept His message. His statement about a prophet being honored everywhere except in His own home found graphic fulfillment in His immediate family, since even His own brothers, including James, would not come to believe in Him until after His resurrection (John 7:5; Mark 3:21; 1 Cor 15:7).

Jesus then referred to the incidents of Elijah's being sent to the Gentile Sidonian woman (1 Kgs 17:9–24) and Elisha's healing of the Gentile Naaman (2 Kgs 5). His point was that these prophets were *not* sent to Israelites but to Gentiles. The stunning application was that if Israel was unworthy to receive His message, then God would send His prophet elsewhere—even if it was to the Gentiles! He knew that His own hometown crowd would not accept the message intended for them, but many Gentiles would later accept that same message. His unflattering application was not received with gratefulness by His hearers.

> And all *the people* in the synagogue were filled with rage as they heard these things, and they stood up and drove Him out of the city, and led Him to the edge of the hill on which their city had been built, in order to throw Him down the cliff. But passing through their midst, He went on His way (Luke 4:28–30).

Today you can visit, just south of Nazareth, the top of a sheer cliff that drops over 500 feet to the floor of the Jezreel Valley. While it is difficult to be dogmatic, it is still referred to in popular local tradition as that "precipice" where Jesus' fellow townsmen attempted to provide the young preacher with an unorthodox "reception" following the service!

Although their efforts to kill the brash young "preacher boy" failed, their reaction does indicate a sober truth. No greater blindness exists than among those who refuse to admit that they are blind. While Nazareth was the place of His youth, it did not become the eventual headquarters for Jesus' ministry. That distinction was reserved for little Capernaum, a fishing village on the northern shore of the Sea of Galilee (Luke 4:31ff.), where He soon set up His "headquarters" and also where He performed so many of His miracles. The only record of miraculous deeds in Nazareth is the almost passing comment that He just "healed a few sick people" (Mark 6:5).

This amazing incident comes to life when we see it against its Jewish cultural and historical setting. The electricity of the incident cannot be adequately captured on paper. It must have been humbling for an older resident of Nazareth to be confronted by the kid down the street with such a momentous message. How often pride, ethnic or spiritual, keeps us from receiving what the Lord has for us. Jesus had to go elsewhere to find a receptive audience.

Jesus once told a parable about some seed that, when sown by the wayside, was snatched up by the birds and never took root. Other seeds, however, fell on good ground, took root, and bore fruit (Matt 13:3–9). When Jesus sowed the seed of His Word that day in Nazareth, the wicked one soon snatched it away (Matt 13:19). But other good ground, as small as it was, still awaited the sowing of the Messiah's seed. May we be among those who hear Jesus' Word, receive it, understand it, and bear fruit from it.

▼

Few scholars have explored the exciting field of intertextuality to the degree of Richard B. Hays in his *Echoes of Scripture in the Gospels* (Baylor Press, 2016).

Another helpful book that places Jesus within the Jewish world of the first century is *Jesus and His World* by Craig A. Evans (John Knox Press, 2012).

How can a young man (or woman) keep their way pure?
By keeping *it* according to Your word.
With all my heart I have sought You;
Do not let me stray from Your commandments.
Your word I have treasured in my heart,
That I may not sin against You (Ps 119:9–11, LSB).

Chapter 10

Messiah and Women

It has become fashionable among some feminist writers to castigate Biblical writers for their "sexism" along with terms like "patriarchalism" and "male chauvinism." The entire Judaeo-Christian tradition has often been blamed for perpetuating an unhealthy domination of men over women. A closer examination of the Biblical writers against the background of their contemporary culture, however, reveals quite a different picture. Rather than advocating the oppressive treatment of women, the Biblical authors' attitudes and actions toward women often went against the grain of their contemporary culture and actually helped to eventually elevate the status of women. Christianity in reality helped to upgrade the status of women. The purpose of this chapter is to examine an example of this truly *"liberating"* attitude: the teaching and actions of Jesus in regard to the women whom He encountered in His ministry.

Messiah and Ruth

I had originally planned the following study of Ruth as a separate chapter, but it fits better as a sort of preface to this chapter because it helps us to understand the Old Testament backdrop to Jesus' attitude toward women.

The little account contained in the Book of Ruth has all the elements of an absorbing short story. The reader is exposed to a plot containing elements of family, tragedy, conflict, characterization, and resolution. The action moves to a truly satisfying, not artificial, "they lived happily ever after" conclusion. Literary critics have appreciated this little book relating a story with a happy ending during a period of many unhappy endings—the period of the Judges (Ruth 1:1). One can also approach the book as the third part of a "Bethlehem Trilogy." The first two parts come at the end of Judges, in that truly awful account of a man twice leaving Bethlehem and then experiencing awful behavior that could be viewed as bringing shame on that little town. Likewise, in the third part of the Trilogy, a man named Elimelech leaves Bethlehem with his wife Naomi and two sons. Great pain ensues with the deaths of the father and both sons, leaving Naomi and two women as widows. Here we go again, one might say! But the rest of this wonderful little book is an amazing account about the pain of two women turned to joy, the reputation of Bethlehem rescued, and all this through the role of a *goel* or Kinsman-Redeemer.

As a reader finished this enchanting idyll he or she may, however, be let down by the last five verses of the book, which seem to be a rather pedantic afterthought. The verses comprise a genealogical list of ten generations—six before Boaz and Ruth and three following the happy couple.

Now these are the generations of Perez: Perez fathered Hezron, Hezron fathered Ram, Ram fathered Amminadab, Amminadab fathered Nahshon, Nahshon fathered Salmon, Salmon fathered Boaz, Boaz fathered Obed, Obed fathered Jesse, and Jesse fathered David (Ruth 4:18–22).

Why would this apparently boring roster be appended to such a beautiful, engaging and romantic tale? Because all of God's Word is "God-breathed" and "profitable" (2 Tim 3:16–17), we must reflect on what this conclusion of the book is communicating to us.

When we begin reading the New Testament, we are confronted with a similar *shock*. Instead of immediately launching into the account of Jesus' birth, Matthew serves us 17 verses, containing nearly 50 names, covering a period of almost 2,000 years (Matt 1:1–17)! Many readers admittedly skip over this list of unfamiliar characters so they can get to the *good stuff* in verse 18 and following. By ignoring this small paragraph, however, they miss some fascinating truths. As a matter of fact, the genealogies at the conclusion of Ruth and at the beginning of Matthew are strikingly similar. It even appears that Matthew consciously adapted the end of Ruth in his own register of Jesus' ancestors. What did the Spirit of God desire to teach us by including these name lists at such crucial places in His inspired Word?

One of the striking facets of Jesus' genealogy in Matthew is its inclusion of women, quite uncharacteristic of ancient Jewish genealogies. No less than four are mentioned, three by name and one by her relationship to her husband. The first is *Tamar* (Matt 1:3), who gave birth to Perez by Judah (Genesis 38). The second is *Rahab* (Matt 1:5), who gave birth to Boaz by Salmon (Ruth 4:21). The third is *Ruth* (Matt 1:5), who gave birth to Obed by Boaz (Ruth 4:21). The fourth is *Bathsheba* ("her that had been the wife of Uriah" (Matt 1:6), who gave birth to Solomon by David (2 Sam 12:24).

The following table helps to visualize better the parallels between the two genealogies:

Matthew 1:3–6	Ruth 4:18–22
"Judah begot **Perez** ...of **Tamar**" (1:3)	"**Perez**" (4:18)
"**Salmon** begot Boaz of **Rahab**" (1:5)	"**Salmon**" (4:20)
"**Boaz** begot Obed of **Ruth**" (1:5)	"**Boaz**" (4:21)
"**David**, the king, begot Solomon of her that had been the **wife** of Uriah" (1:6)	"**David**" (4:22)

The purpose of Ruth's genealogy is to show that her husband Boaz was a descendant of Judah, the man who fathered the tribe of the King-Messiah (Gen 49:10). Furthermore, it indicates that Ruth was the great-grandmother of David, the man God chose to be king (1 Sam 16:12) and the ancestor of the Messiah.

The purpose of Matthew's genealogy is to record the messianic line down to Joseph, whom Matthew is careful to show was not the physical father of Jesus, but His *legal,* adoptive father: "And Jacob was the father of Joseph the husband of Mary, by whom Jesus was born, who is called Christ (the Messiah)" (Matt 1:16).

Further reflection on Matthew's inclusion of these four women presents some other striking paradoxes. Not only did he include women in the ancestry of the Messiah but there were other *negative* aspects of these women that stand out. They were all *Gentiles or related in some way to a Gentile*: Tamar and Rahab were Canaanites; Ruth was a Moabite; and Bathsheba was married to the Gentile, Uriah the Hittite. As if that were not enough, each of these women had some shadow over her behavior or background. Tamar and Rahab had been prostitutes; Bathsheba had committed adultery; and Ruth was a member of a people who were ancient enemies of Israel and whose men were excluded from the congregation of the Lord for ten generations (Deut 23:3). If you or I had written Jesus' genealogy, we would perhaps have been tempted to omit these questionable female "Gentiles" from the list. But Matthew, without apology or fear of embarrassment, portrayed them for us all to read and to recognize. Is there a reason for this inclusion?

I believe that the reason relates to why the little story of Ruth is included in the Bible. Ruth was a Gentile woman who was the great-grandmother of the greatest king of Israel, David. This indicates God's love and grace to this dear woman. What a privilege to be included in the ancestry of the "sweet psalmist of Israel" (2 Sam 23:1), the son of Judah through whom a great covenant was made that declared that the Messiah would be one of his descendants (2 Sam 7:14; Luke 1:32). So it is with the larger picture of the four women included in the genealogy of Jesus by Matthew. Perhaps what the Lord is showing to us here at the beginning of the New Testament is that:

1. Jesus is also for *women*, not just for men. This truth, echoed so often in the Gospels (they were last at the cross and first at the tomb), ought to encourage every female follower of the Savior.

2. Jesus is also for *Gentiles*, not just for Jews. Their inclusion here previewed the eventual inclusion of those "other sheep" (John 10:16) that Jesus would call, who are outside the fold of Israel.

3. Jesus is also for *sinners*, not just for the righteous. Did not Jesus Himself state this very truth in Matt 9:13b, "I did not come to call the righteous, but sinners"?

I can imagine an aged Ruth called one happy day to the home of her grandson, Jesse. There her dim eyes beheld a red-headed newborn—the eighth son of Jesse. When she attended his circumcision and heard him named "David," did she recognize that this little one would be the ancestor of the Messiah who would be the "Lion of the Tribe of Judah" (Rev 5:5) and who would one day take the throne of His father David (Luke 1:32)? She had already experienced redemption by a *goel*—her beloved "redeemer," Boaz. Perhaps she recognized that an even greater Redeemer would come someday from her very own seed. She must have been grateful that she, a Gentile Moabite woman, was privileged to be included in the line of the Messianic King. This is what is conveyed to us by that "boring" list of ten names in Ruth 4:18–22.

Women in Ancient Judaism

What was it like then to be a woman in ancient Israel? During the Old Testament period, women were relieved from some responsibilities. For example, they were exempt from the requirement to attend the annual festivals (Exod 23:17), but they were allowed to do so if they were able (1 Sam 1:9, 21–22). The Mosaic Law recognized that wives and mothers would have responsibilities in the home that made public attendance at religious gatherings difficult. On the other hand, women were able to serve at the door of the tabernacle (Exod 38:8); to take the Nazirite vow along with men (Num 6:2); to hear the Word of God along with men (Neh 8:2–3); to engage in music ministry along with men (Exod 15:20, 21); and sometimes even to prophesy along with men (Exod 15:20; Judg 4:6–7; 2 Kgs 22:14; Neh 6:14). It is clear, however, that the office of priest was limited to male members of the priestly line (Exod 28:1; Num 18:1–7). Other than this restriction from the priesthood, there was far more freedom for women than is often thought.

It was in the centuries following the close of the Old Testament that the rabbis instituted practices that went beyond the

Biblical norms and resulted in greater restriction of women's privileges. These rabbinical strictures were not divinely inspired and often reflect a wrong attitude toward women and their abilities, and should not be identified with Biblical commands or practices. Rabbinical writings in the Mishna and Talmud reflect practices that were contemporary with the time of Jesus' earthly ministry. The following four social norms were practiced in Jesus' day.

1. *Women were to be shunned in public social contact.* Consider the following passage from the *Mishna* tractate *Abot*, 1.5: "Engage not in too much conversation with women. They said this with regard to one's own wife. How much more does the rule apply to another man's wife. As long as a man engages in too much conversation with women, he causes evil to himself, for he goes idle from the study of the Torah, so that his end will be that he will inherit gehenna."

2. *Women were not to be publicly taught the Torah.* This was *not* true in the Old Testament period (Josh 8:35; Neh 8:2–3). Consider, however, the following passage from the tractate *Sota*, 10a: "May the words of Torah be burned, than that they should be handed over to women." This attitude about women's innate inability to learn the Torah was manifested in having special "*courts*" for women in the Second Temple and also in synagogues, separated from the men. The latter practice has continued until today among the Orthodox. The idea that they could learn in the same schools with men was not even entertained during the Second Temple Period.

3. *Women were restricted from orally communicating the Torah to others, even to children.* Consider *Mishna Kiddushin* 4.13: "An unmarried man must not be a teacher of children, nor may a woman be a teacher of children." This restriction applied also to publicly reading Scripture in the synagogue (Megillot 73a) and even to pronouncing the benediction after a meal in the home (*Mishna Bereshit* 7:2).

4. *Women had no right to bear public witness in a judicial case.* *Baba Kamma* 88a declares, "Though the woman is subject to the commandments, she is disqualified from giving evidence." The first century Jewish historian, Josephus, characterized the general attitude of his time in *Antiquities* 4.219: "Let not the testimony of women be admitted because of the levity and boldness of their sex."

Such burdensome restrictions certainly went far beyond what the Old Testament taught about a woman's role outside the home. The Rabbinic Judaism of the first century actually involved more reaction than progress. When viewed against this rigid background, the attitude of Jesus toward women in His ministry comes as a breath of fresh air!

Women in Jesus' Teaching and Actions

In His public teaching, Jesus never uttered a word of deprecation regarding women. They never were the butt of cruel jokes nor were they ever "put down" for being women. In His condemnation of adultery and divorce in Matt 5:27–28 and 19:3–10, He taught that women were not to be treated as *sex objects*. In His sermons, He twice used the example of a woman to rebuke the faithless men of His generation—the widow of Zarephath to the men of Nazareth in Luke 4:28–29 and the Queen of Sheba to the Pharisees in Luke 11:31. At least twice in His parables, Jesus used a woman in a striking way to illustrate faith and determination: the persistent widow in Luke 18:2–8 and the woman searching for the lost coin in Luke 15:8–10.

Jesus never uttered any word that would support the idea of treating women as inferior to men. They were always honored in His teaching and never humiliated—a practice modern preachers should follow! In many churches today, women often endure cruel comments at their expense—something Jesus never did.

It was not only in what He taught, but also in how He related to women publicly that Jesus displayed a truly *revolutionary* attitude—in the sense that He was overthrowing the *wrong* social conventions of His day. Consider the following three incidents in His ministry, each of which involved a woman.

1. Jesus' very public ministry to the *Samaritan woman* at a well in John 4:1–42 contravened *"accepted"* practice for a Jewish male of His day. He not only talked to the woman in public, He instructed her and revealed Himself to her as the Messiah! The disciples' astonishment at Jesus' action is indicated in John 4:27: "And at this point His disciples came, and they were marveling that He was speaking with a woman, yet no one said, 'What do You seek?' or, 'Why are You speaking with her?'" Jesus simply disobeyed the Rabbinic restriction against public speaking with a woman. He always sought to minister to women, not ignore them, even if it meant risking the misunderstanding of His own male disciples.

2. The case of the *woman taken in adultery* (John 7:53–8:11) provides another example of His compassionate attitude to women. Jesus rebuked her accusers who had conveniently ignored the guilty man! While not approving of her action ("Go, and from now on sin no more," 8:11), His tender dealing with her contrasted sharply with the harsh and hypocritical attitude of those who were so quick to pronounce the sentence of death upon her.

3. The incident in the house of *Mary and Martha* (Luke 10:38–42) provides another example of Jesus not following *"accepted"* social norms of His day about instructing women. Not only did He instruct Mary, His words to Martha indicate that Mary had actually chosen the better part. While Jesus would never have condemned a woman for attending to household duties, He still commended Mary for desiring to study and learn the Word. The rabbis thought women intellectually inferior and incapable of study—Jesus evidently thought otherwise.

Woman with a hemorrhage touching Jesus' garment. Photograph of painting in Magdala

4. A woman with a flow of blood for twelve years reached out in a crowd to touch the tassel on His outer garment (Luke 8:43–47). In addition to these incidents in His ministry, note that it was a woman to whom Jesus chose to reveal Himself first after His resurrection (Mary Magdalene in Luke 24:1-10). Women were the last ones at the cross, when all of the male disciples but John forsook their Master and fled! They were also the first ones at the tomb, when those same males were cowering in fear. It was a woman Jesus chose to be the first witness to His resurrection and then He commissioned her to testify to its truth! The rabbis did not believe women were reliable witnesses. Do not miss the reaction of the men when they heard this testimony of the women, "But these words appeared to them as nonsense, and they were not believing them" (Luke 24:11).

It is no wonder that Jesus had such a positive impact on women, who were often neglected by the teachers of that period. Luke 8:1-3 tells us that many women followed Him and ministered to His needs. Why is it that a formerly immoral woman could cry tears of thanks on Jesus' feet and dry them with her hair without fear of rebuke? (Luke 7:38). Why is it that Mary felt so free in His presence and would anoint His feet with costly perfume, even risking rebuke by others (John 12:3)? It is because the Master simply accepted these women as persons. Compassionately and with complete purity He accepted their affection while moving them to repentance.

The Christian novelist, essayist and scholar, Dorothy Sayers remarked incisively,

> They had never known a man like this Man; there never has been such another. A prophet and teacher who never nagged at them nor patronized them; who never made jokes about them and who took their questions seriously; who took them as He found them. Nobody could possibly guess from the words and deeds of Jesus that there was anything 'funny' about woman's nature (*Are Women Human?*, 47).

It is important also to notice that Jesus did *not* choose women as His apostles, a practice consistent with the later Pauline instruction that the authoritative teaching function in the church is the responsibility of men (1 Tim 2:11–15). This restriction, however, does not mean that women were second class citizens in the church! A vast number of roles are open to them both within and outside the church. Where would the average church be today without Godly women?

Wherever the Gospel has penetrated the cultures of this world, an inevitable result has been that the social status of women has been lifted. Look at the oppressive plight of women in countries where Islam is allowed to define their role. Rather than attack Christianity for oppressing women, we need to recognize that the message of the Gospel provides true spiritual "liberation" for both males and females.

The Apostle Paul had female co-workers without fear of condemnation. "I urge Euodia and I urge Syntyche to think the same way in the Lord. Indeed, I ask you also, genuine companion, help these women who have contended together alongside of me in the gospel, with also Clement and the rest of my fellow workers, whose names are in the book of life" (Phil 4:2–3). This same apostle, often derided as a misogynist, has expressed his attitude beautifully and without contradiction, "There is neither Jew nor Greek, there is neither slave nor free man, there is no male and female, for you are all one in Christ Jesus" (Gal 3:28).

Was Jesus, therefore, a "feminist?" Certainly He was not a feminist the way that word is defined today. He simply was one who taught women's true liberation through the power of the truth as revealed in the Gospel.

Lower Galilee was the main area of Jesus' Jewish ministry. Here a number of women followed Jesus and supported Him and His disciples (Luke 8:1–3)

 For a readable treatment of the ministry of women throughout the Bible see the author's *To Preach or Not to Preach: Women's Ministry Then and Now* (2018).

O Messiah who loves all men and women the same, grant to my sisters in the faith to know You more clearly, to love You more dearly and to follow You more nearly. Through Jesus our Messiah, the Savior of all. Amen.

Chapter 11

Messiah and the Goyim

The word *Goyim* in the title may not be familiar to you. It simply means "Gentiles" or non-Jews. Sometimes it is rendered as "nations," but that sounds too political to convey the ancient meaning of goyim. The single word "goy" means a non-Jew or simply a Gentile.

I want to begin this chapter by attempting to disabuse you of two ideas that are widespread, at least among many Christians. The first misconception has to do with the people who were the primary target of each Gospel, especially the Gospel of Matthew. Sometimes we summarize the purpose of each Gospel with the following general paradigm. Matthew was written for the Jews; Mark was written for the Romans; Luke was written for the Greeks; and John was written for the world. Now you may or may not have heard it expressed in those very words. I must confess in my early years of teaching the life of Jesus the Messiah, I also may have described the target audience of the Gospels in that way. There is some truth in those summaries but the whole truth is much more nuanced. I was wrong in this opinion. That is what studying the Bible does sometimes. It often shatters your previous conceptions.

The second idea is that although Jesus came for the Jews and the Gospel was initially for the Jews, after Israel as a whole refused to receive Jesus as Messiah, God turned to the Gentiles with the hope that they would receive it. They were more receptive so the Gospel for them was a sort of Christianity 2.0. The Jews rejected Christianity 1.0 so stage 2.0 went into effect in its place. Now nobody says it exactly in that way, but you ought to admit that you have thought about it that way, at least at one point in your life. I want to deal with that issue secondly in this chapter. I want to argue that from the beginning Christianity 1.0 had no other plan in case it initially did not work out with the Jewish people. Gentiles were part of the Divine plan for the Gospel from the beginning.

The purpose of this chapter on "Messiah and the Goyim" is to present a more robust and accurate picture of where the Gentiles fit into the Messiah's plans and how the Old Testament's Messianic Hope was planned for and portrayed in the Gospels, the Acts, and the Epistles. We begin by focusing on the Gentiles in the Gospels, especially the Gospel of Matthew.

Upon first examination, we can see why people might think that Matthew is focusing his primary attention on the Jews. Old Testament quotations are all over the place. (Nobody said "Old Testament" in those days but you know what I mean: it is those 39 books written in Hebrew and Aramaic and anciently translated into Greek in the Septuagint; it is the group of books that begin with Genesis and end with Malachi, well at least in our English Bible, but that is another story). But now back to how "Jewish" the first Gospel really looks. As I said, we admit that at first glance Matthew surely looks like the Jews are the leading characters of the show in this book. The initial genealogy in Matthew appears to be an all-star list of Old Testament Jewish heroes. We soon see the Jewish prophet Isaiah quoted and then Micah and then Hosea and then Jeremiah. This all is taking place in a very Jewish land, namely the "land of Israel" (Matt 2:21). We encounter Jewish religious leaders like Pharisees and Sadducees and Jewish synagogues. While all that is true, we need to look closer to see how important a place the Gentiles have in Matthew's account.

Scholars use the word *inclusio* as a literary term for what we sometimes mean by the word "bookends." It is defined as a similar word or idea that begins and ends a literary work. Matthew carefully crafts his Gospel by using the Gentiles as an *inclusio* that begins and ends his work. Look at the closing words of the Gospel: "Go therefore and make disciples of all the nations (Gentiles), baptizing them in the name of the Father and the Son and the Holy Spirit, teaching them to keep all that I commanded you; and behold, I am with you always, even to the end of the age" (Matt 28:19–20). We know it as the Great Commission, and the command to these Jewish disciples is to disciple the Gentiles. Shift back to the beginning of Matthew and you find what looks like a very Jewish genealogy of Jesus. He is a descendant of Abraham and David (1:1) and then come the descendants of Abraham who are carefully traced down to Joseph, the legal father of Jesus, whom Matthew also shows is the physical son of Mary not Joseph (1:16). Now genealogies in the Bible trace descent through the fathers, not the mothers, but Matthew's genealogy is different. He includes four women who were the wives of those males: Tamar (1:3), Rahab (1:5), Ruth (1:5), and Bathsheba whom he calls "the wife of Uriah" (1:6). Readers of the Old Testament will recall these women also had some moral shadow hanging over their behavior, but also at least three of these ancestresses of Jesus were Gentiles. It appears that Bathsheba was Jewish, although she was married to a Gentile, Uriah the Hittite. So at the beginning and at the end of this so-called "Jewish Gospel," and forming a sort of "Goyim Inclusio," are Gentiles—some in the ancestry of the Messiah and others as future disciples of this Jewish

The "Mount of Beatitudes," traditional site of the Sermon on the Mount

Messiah. One does not need to read much further in Matthew to discover also the Gentile Magi from the East who come searching for this "King of the Jews" whom they want to worship (2:2). We should not forget that he who was called by Rome a "King of the Jews" (Herod) was *not* present in that Bethlehem house when these Gentile Magi worshipped the Messianic "King of the Jews"! Remember again that Matthew is the only so-called Jewish Gospel that mentions these Gentiles.

A survey of Matthew reveals other times when Gentiles were recipients of the Jewish Messiah's grace. A Gentile is included when Jesus heals the son of the Centurion in Capernaum (8:5–13). Showing not only the Messiah's mercy but foreshadowing that the Gospel will eventually be extended to all peoples. About the Centurion, Jesus says, "Truly I say to you, I have not found such great faith with anyone in Israel. And I say to you that many will come from east and west, and recline *at the table* with Abraham,

Isaac and Jacob in the kingdom of heaven; but the sons of the kingdom will be cast out into the outer darkness; in that place there will be weeping and gnashing of teeth" (Matt 8:10–12). Later Jesus withdraws from the very Jewish land of Israel to what we call today Lebanon and there He encounters the heart-felt plea of a woman who was a descendant of the despised Canaanites! When the Canaanite mother also humbly asserts her claim and displays her faith not by protesting the apparent insult to her people (Jesus alludes to them as "dogs"), Jesus heals her daughter (Matt 15:21–28). In other words, both Gentiles (dogs) and Jews (children) are to be recipients of the Messiah's grace.

As Jesus returns from this withdrawal to a Gentile area, He loops around the north side and then the east side of the Sea of Galilee through the heavily Gentile region known as the Decapolis, a league of ten mostly Gentile cities in modern day Syria and Jordan. During this ministry among Gentiles He healed many (Matt 15:30) and Matthew then includes something unique in the Gospels. "And large crowds came to Him, bringing with them *those who were* lame, crippled, blind, mute, and many others, and they laid them down at His feet; and He healed them. So the crowd marveled as they saw the mute speaking, the crippled restored, and the lame walking, and the blind seeing; and *they glorified the God of Israel*" (15:31). I italicized the words of that last expression to call attention to the fact that these were Gentiles who were praising Israel's God who had sent His Jewish Messiah to bless and to heal them! I include the above texts about Gentile healings because they immediately precede Matthew's account of feeding the four thousand (15:32–38). Most Christians are familiar with Jesus' feeding the Jewish crowd of five thousand (14:13–31), a miracle recorded in all four of the Gospels. But Matthew along with Mark (8:1–10) mention this additional miracle. Since Jesus had not yet returned to Jewish Galilee (15:39), this second miraculous feeding was of a Gentile crowd gathered from the Decapolitan cities.

Hippos, one of the cities of the Gentile Decapolis, on the east shore of the Sea of Galilee

The two feedings, one of a Jewish crowd and one of a Gentile crowd, also fit Matthew's narrative structure. Let us look again at the visit of Jesus to that Gentile woman who humbly took her place as an undeserving descendant of Canaan, the son of Ham (Matt 15:21–28). The incident stands between the two miraculous feedings. Jesus' initially harsh-sounding response that it is not appropriate to throw the (Jewish) children's bread to (Gentile) dogs performs a more significant role than simply as a mean retort. Perhaps her humble response that the dogs will gladly settle for a few crumbs from the table serves as a paradigm for the two feedings. "The children, represented by five thousand Jews, have received their bread, and the dogs, represented by the four thousand Gentiles, now may receive the crumbs falling from the table" (Hussung, "Jesus's Feeding of the Gentiles in Matt 15:29–30," 488).

Some small fish recalling what was left over after the miracle.

If you are not yet convinced that Matthew and Mark record one miraculous feeding of a Jewish crowd and later one of a Gentile crowd, consider two more small but significant facts. Before Jesus distributed the bread to the first group, He "blessed" it (14:19); for the second group He "gave thanks" for it (15:36).

Jews commonly speak of such a prayer as a "blessing," (e.g., Luke 14:30). Gentiles would not be as used to hearing that expression and "thanks" is more appropriate. This is a small difference but it is significant. Last and maybe least is that a different word for the "twelve *baskets*" (*kophinous*) of leftovers is used in the first miracle; the second group of seven baskets is a word that the LSB calls "large baskets" (*spuridas*) to preserve the distinction (Matt 15:37). Again this is not an argument that convinces by itself, but taken together with the other reasons we have given, it supports the idea of two different ethnic groups being fed miraculously.

The loaves and fish as portrayed in an ancient mosaic floor near the site of the miracle

In Matthew's report of the amazing Olivet Discourse, Jesus teaches about the future judgment with the separation of sheep and goats. He declared, "And all the nations (Gentiles) will be gathered before

Him; and He will separate them from one another, as the shepherd separates the sheep from the goats" (25:32). We should be careful to mention that Jesus not only blesses the Gentiles, but that He also holds them accountable for rejecting His person and message.

We have seen that Jesus included the Gentiles, although in a limited way, in His announcement of the Good news, but we still need to deal with the issue raised earlier about whether the early preachers believed that Gentiles were originally included in this Gospel plan. The only way we can tell that is if they employed the Old Testament to justify their evangelistic inclusion of non-Jews. Let us look at the example of the Jewish Apostle Paul, who is sometimes referred to as "the Apostle to the Gentiles." Did he think of this new evangelism of the non-Jews as Christianity 2.0? Look at his surprising use of an Old Testament text from Isaiah when He was preaching in the Jewish synagogue in Antioch. When word got around town that these two Jewish newcomers (Paul and Barnabas) were in town giving a message that might include them, they pressed into the synagogue, which did not make the Jewish attenders very happy (Acts 13:44–45). Let's allow Luke to tell the rest of this exciting story.

> Paul and Barnabas spoke out boldly and said, "It was necessary that the word of God be spoken to you first. Since you reject it and judge yourselves unworthy of eternal life, behold, we are turning to the Gentiles. For so the Lord has commanded us, 'I have placed You as a light for the Gentiles, That You may bring salvation to the end of the earth.'" And when the Gentiles heard this, they *began* rejoicing and glorifying the word of the Lord, and as many as had been appointed to eternal life believed (Acts 13:46–48).

Paul did not view the inclusion of the Gentiles in this good news as an afterthought. He grounded their inclusion in an important text from the Jewish prophet Isaiah. As the Servant Messiah (Jesus) was prophesied by Isaiah, His servant Paul was fulfilling that mission as well in opening the door of faith to those outside the family of Israel. And all of this was grounded in a very Jewish Old Testament Messianic promise.

We conclude our chapter on Messiah and the Goyim by citing an often overlooked and ignored passage from Paul's letter to the Romans, chapter 15. Many Protestant Evangelicals overlook this passage toward the end of the book because we strongly affirm the earlier expressed doctrine of justification by faith, which was also based on an Old Testament statement (Hab 2:4)! While we should affirm that important Gospel truth, we should not forget that the overlooked theme in Romans is the acceptance of Gentiles into the faith in the same way as the Jews. Paul had said early on that the Gospel was to the Jew first and also to the Greek (1:16), but was this only because the Jews had largely rejected this message? Paul will answer "no" quite loudly in this neglected section of Romans. Truly the key to this house of Romans is found near the back door! Paul can say it better than I can.

> Therefore, accept one another, just as the Messiah also accepted us to the glory of God. For I say that the Messiah has become a servant to the circumcision on behalf of the truth of God to confirm the promises *given* to the fathers, and for the Gentiles to glorify God for His mercy; as it is written,
>
> "Therefore I will give praise to You among the Gentiles,
> And I will sing to Your name."
> And again he says,
> "Rejoice, O Gentiles, with His people."
> And again,
> "Praise the Lord all you Gentiles,
> And let all the peoples praise Him."

And again Isaiah says,
"There shall come the root of Jesse,
And He who arises to rule over the Gentiles,
In Him shall the Gentiles hope" (Rom 15:7-12).

The apostle bases the reception of believing Gentiles into the family of God not on some pragmatic decision but on the Old Testament promises that are drawn from all sections of that "Jewish" Bible! Those texts are Ps 19:49 (15:9); Deut 32:43 (15:10); Ps 117:1 (15:11); and Isa 11:10 (15:12). This is the overlooked theme of Romans, that Gentiles are accepted on the same basis as believing Jews, and it is through that way of faith because the Old Testament Scriptures stated it clearly!

Then what did the often-quoted statement by Jesus to the Canaanite woman mean: "I am sent only to the house of Israel" (Matt 15:24)? This is certainly true, but it is obvious that when desperate and sick and weary Gentiles approached Jesus, He always welcomed them, as He did this Gentile woman. When Gentiles began attending the synagogue to hear this message, Paul welcomed them! The Old Testament covenant was promised to Israel, but when Gentiles like Rahab and Ruth wanted to enter, they were not turned away.

This Gentile boy from South Carolina is also very thankful that I was welcomed by Jesus into this "Jewish family"—simply by faith!

▼

 A valuable commentary on Matthew is the one volume edition of *Matthew: A Shorter Commentary*, Dale C. Allison, Jr., ed. (T&T Clark, 2004). I am also indebted in this chapter to Benjamin Hussung, "Jesus's Feeding of the Gentiles in Matt 15:29-30," *Journal of the Evangelical Theological Society*, 63.3 (2020): 473-89.

O Father, I pray that the various peoples and nations and tongues of this earth will glorify the Lamb that was slain. May riches and glory and honor be to the Lamb that was slain. Amen.

Chapter 12

Messiah and the Madman

I had not planned to include a chapter on this event, but an inquiry on my Facebook page, Nerdy Bible Language Majors, made me reconsider after I thought I had finished the manuscript! Today the man delivered in this story would be called insane or a madman (hence the title), but the Gospels are clear that this was a case of Jesus delivering a man possessed not by one demon but by possibly over a thousand evil spirits! This is one of those events in Jesus' life and ministry where all three of the Synoptic Gospels come together (Matt 8:28–34; Mark 5:1–20; Luke 8:26–39). The following Scripture references are from the Markan account unless they are otherwise noted.

Knowing the location of this miracle is important for understanding this amazing series of events. Undoubtedly, everything took place on the shore of the Sea of Galilee. The "other side" of the sea (5:1, 21) was on the eastern shore of what really is a freshwater lake, 12 miles long and six miles wide. We also know that it was near the Decapolis (5:20), a league of ten Greek cities. The Gospels describe the "country" or "region" with three different names. Early manuscripts are divided between the readings

The eastern shore of the Sea of Galilee near the site where the "Madman" was delivered

"Gergasenes," "Gadarenes," and "Gerasenes." Both Gadara and Gerasa (modern Jerash) are a good distance from the Sea of Galilee, with the former about five miles southeast and the latter over twenty miles further. The details of the account demand a location having a hillside that slopes steeply into the sea (5:13), and Gergasa is the only place that meets this requirement. The going "away" of the delivered man and his preaching "in the Decapolis" (5:20) fits Gergasa because it is not part of the Decapolis, whereas both Gadara and Gerasa would not require any departure from the region (Matt 8:34). Greek scribes would find it easy to substitute the better-known cities of Gadara and Gerasa for the more obscure Gergasa. The modern location, called Kursi in Arabic, may even be a corruption of Gergasa. One Gospel mentions that people came from "the city" (5:33–34), and one of the Decapolis cities, Hippos, is on the eastern shore. The final geographical feature that helps us locate this site is that there is a previously mentioned slope down which the pigs ran that is immediately north of Hippos! Therefore, my suggestion is that the miracle took place just north of that slope (Kursi), a locale commemorated today by a ruined Byzantine chapel, built probably into the ancient tomb.

If there is disagreement on the precise location of these events, all agree that this is one of the most dramatic Jesus-encounters in the Gospels! The demoniac was yelling night and day and lacerating himself, which not only indicates his awful torments but illustrates the goal of the possessing spirit(s) to utterly destroy his life. The dramatic encounter builds up to a climactic struggle, not between the demoniac and Jesus but between Jesus and the many demons whom He was confronting. Notice the seemingly contradictory switch from a singular to a plural when Jesus asks the demon's name: "**My** name is Legion; for **we** are many" (5:9). He even calls himself by the name, "Legion," and a Roman legion normally consisted of at least 6,000 soldiers. Jesus has proven Himself stronger than demons before (1:39; 3:22), but the unusual physical power of this demoniac is indicated by (1) the inability of anyone to bind him; (2) the uselessness of shackles on his hands, feet, and legs; (3) the failure of many past attempts to control him; and (4) his having grown stronger so no one could subdue him. This confrontation, however, will be the biggest test thus far of Jesus' Messianic authority and power.

"Usually, adjuring occurs in formulas of exorcism, so that by using this verb the unclean spirit is trying to turn the tables on Jesus by exorcising him out of the region, and in the attempt is using the most potent name possible, 'God,' short for 'the Most High God,' which immediately precedes" (Gundry, *Commentary on the New Testament*, 156). This unclean spirit somehow knows that he and his hordes are dealing with Jesus, the Son of the Living God. The spirit(s) had not yet come out even though Jesus had commanded it (them) to do so. The spirit launches a counter-attack, but the greater the difficulty faced, so the greater will be the Messiah's victory. Jesus gains the advantage over them by demanding that the demoniac reveal his name, which was also their name: Legion! When they "realize that resistance is futile," they request to be cast out of the man, begging Jesus not to send them outside the region, but into a group of pigs nearby. The spirits had almost succeeded in destroying the life of the poor human being who had suffered for so many years. Now they succeed in an effort to destroy the lives of their swine hosts, and also the livelihood of their owner!

A steep slope down to the water near the site of the miracle

Years ago, I heard a preacher say that this "Jewish pig farmer" deserved what he got in losing his herd because he had no business raising what are non-kosher unclean animals! Such an uninformed comment forgets that this account is not set in a Jewish area (the west side of the lake) but in what was Gentile territory (the east side of the lake)! Another thoroughly modern observation is the criticism from those who considered themselves politically correct liberals who opine that Jesus was so heartlessly cruel to destroy the lives of these helpless animals. Such a comment indicates how upside-down our world has become when people can show more concern for animals than for the life of pain suffered by this poor man, who had just been delivered from that misery by a miracle of Divine power!

The people of the region and probably those from the city next door, Hippos, plead with Jesus to leave, probably because they feared more losses in the future like that of the pig farmer's business if Jesus continued these acts of deliverance. "The awesome power of Jesus leads them to implore him just as the unclean spirits had implored him and imploring him to leave their borders recollects those spirits' trying to exorcise him out of their region" (Gundry, *Commentary on the New Testament*, 157).

Out of deeply grateful love, the delivered man then desires to join Jesus as He and His disciples board their boat at the end of what was a very busy day (Mark 4:1–5:20)! What better place for a man to be, who certainly needed some "follow up" ministry, than among this Godly group! But Jesus implores him with a far different request than before. "'Go home to your people and report to them what great things the **Lord** has done for you, and *how* He had mercy on you.' And he went away and began to preach in the Decapolis what great things **Jesus** had done for him; and everyone was marveling" (5:19–20). Do not miss in these two verses the subtle but clear equation of what the Lord does with what Jesus does. See Mark 1:2–3 for another identification of the Lord with Jesus.

Jesus has shown abundant mercy to Gentiles during this segment of His Great Galilean Ministry. This is another example of Jesus' never turning away anyone when they had a need, even if they were not from the family of Israel. Although it is not the time yet to add a Gentile to the Twelve Apostles, this man still was given a commission, and he fulfilled it by telling all he encountered about what this Jewish Messiah had done for this probably Gentile "madman." Here is a God who never abandons anyone, no matter how 'far gone' they seem to be. Here is a Jesus who acts with authority over all the forces that rear their ugly heads in this world. Here is a spiritual power who can transform the saddest and most frightening of human situations. This is what it is like when God takes charge.

Here there is also a lesson for us today. The saying goes that there is no better advertisement for a product than a satisfied customer. You may not have been to Bible college, but if the Lord has blessed and delivered you; if He has been faithful to you; and if He has done great things for you, then go out and tell others about it all. And may the effect of your witness be the same as that of these Gentile hearers. "And everyone was marveling" (5:20). May it be!

------▼------

The valuable work by Robert Gundry, *Commentary on the New Testament* (Baker Academic, 2010), is a goldmine of concisely expressed insights and has been very helpful in writing this chapter.

Grant us, good Lord, to reach out for Your help no matter how unbelievably difficult things may seem. Give us Your blessing and Your hope at every level we live and in every moment we breathe. Our Messiah, please deliver us from Satan and sin and sadness. In Your name I pray. Amen.

Chapter 13

Messiah's Metamorphosis

An explanation of this title is needed. Two of the Gospel writers in their accounts use a verb that is translated "transfigure" to describe what happened to Jesus on that mountain. The verb is the root of the later scientific word, *metamorphosis*, used for the "transfiguration" of a caterpillar into a butterfly. Later Greek church fathers used this noun form of the verb to describe the transfiguration. It was a *metamorphosis* of Jesus' earthly appearance into a glorified form. All three of the Synoptic Gospels record this obviously vital event and two of the disciples present refer to it later in their writings (John 1:14 and 2 Peter 1:17–18). This experience stamped itself in the psyches and hearts of these men, and they wrote graphically about it. The third apostle present on that day, John's brother James, did not live long enough to describe it in writing for us (Acts 12:2). As in a previous chapter, I will first explain the facts about this event and then will try to draw out the amazing theological significance of the Messiah's "Metamorphosis" or Transfiguration.

I have mentioned before that there are only a few events in the life of our Messiah before His passion that are described by all four of the Gospel writers. One is the feeding of the five thousand. There are also only a few extended events that are mentioned by all three Synoptists. Two of these are (1) the ministry of John the Baptist in his baptism of Jesus and (2) the Transfiguration of Jesus in the presence of Peter, James, and John. That fact by itself indicates the absolutely essential importance of this event in the life and ministry of our Messiah. This experience is also the second of three times that Peter, James, and John are mentioned as being with Jesus for an important event (see also Mark 5:37 and 14:33). Immediately prior to the Transfiguration Jesus had made a perplexing statement that there were some standing with Him who would not die before they saw His glory (Matt 16:28; Mark 9:1; Luke 9:27). This certainly applies to the three seeing Jesus robed in the glory that He will share at His second coming. In other words, the Transfiguration is a foretaste of that eschatological glory. Peter seems to have understood that meaning in his recollection of this event. "For we did not make known to you the power and **coming** of our Lord Jesus Christ, following cleverly devised myths, but being eyewitnesses of His majesty" (2 Peter 1:16).

The Transfiguration thus follows the confession by Peter that Jesus is the Messiah at Caesarea Philippi. In *Passionate about the Passion Week*, I suggest that the *Via Dolorosa*, the traditional "way of sorrows" that pilgrims walk in Jerusalem, actually began (spiritually) at Caesarea Philippi since it was there that Jesus first clearly taught that He would suffer and die in Jerusalem (Matt 17:21). Because the Transfiguration then takes place after these events, it is appropriate to inquire about the identity of this mountain. Since Byzantine times, a series of churches that commemorate this event have been located on the Biblical Mount Tabor in the Jezreel Valley. Although this place was significant in Old Testament times (Judges 4–5), it is too far away and not high enough (less than a thousand feet) to qualify for the "high mountain" mentioned by Matthew and Mark. Most modern commentators have opted for Mount Hermon, which is located just above Caesarea Philippi. In this writer's opinion, however, it may be too high, around 9000 feet, to imagine this group of four hiking even part of the way to its top. The elapsing of about a week (Matt 17:1; Mark 9:2), suggests that the group had time to go to another mountain on their return to Galilee (Matt 17:22–24). While I am almost alone in this opinion, perhaps Mount Meron is a better choice, since it is high enough but manageable (4000 feet) and it is on their way as they would have returned south to Capernaum.

Caesarea Philippi and Mount Hermon

All accounts of this majestic scene mention the presence with Jesus of the two Old Testament worthies, Moses and Elijah. Why particularly these two? A common answer is that each could be viewed as a representative of the Law and of the Prophets. But since Elijah was not a writing prophet, he would not be representative of that group of canonical prophets from Isaiah through Malachi. A better answer would be that these two luminaries are the

Mt Tabor, traditional site of the Transfiguration, as seen from the Nazareth Ridge

last two people mentioned at the very end of the Old Testament (Mal 4:4–5). They thus could be viewed as anticipating the future hope of the Messiah. This is more probable, but I am convinced by Robert Gundry's suggestion: "these two are the only Old Testament figures to have seen a theophany on a mountain!" (*Matthew*, 343). How appropriate that the cloud surrounding Jesus has all the appearances of an Old Testament theophany. Thus here we also find another evidence of Matthew's Messiah as the new Moses!

The divine voice delivers the powerful message of this event. "While he was still speaking, behold, a bright cloud overshadowed them, and behold, a voice out of the cloud said, "This is My beloved Son, with whom I am well-pleased; listen to Him!" (Matt 17:5). These are the exact words pronounced earlier at the Messiah's baptism, and we will look at those words later in a more in-depth way. I want to point out that this divine statement seems to be in response to Peter's interesting suggestion!

"And Peter answered and said to Jesus, 'Lord, it is good for us to be here; if You wish, I will make three booths here, one for You, and one for Moses, and one for Elijah'" (Matt 17:4). Notice Peter's use of the pronoun "I" in supervising this construction project! The "booths" may be a reference to the practice during the festival of "Tabernacles" or "Booths" commanded in Lev 23:39–43. Did this event take place during the observance of that festival? Or was Peter possibly concluding that the prophecy of an eschatological Festival of Booths in Zech 14:6 was now taking place? Whatever was in the mind of the often impetuously speaking Peter, the presence of the Divine cloud should remind us that "the overshadowing cloud of the divine presence made a covering that was far superior to a tent of branches" (Gundry, *Matthew*, 344).

Having examined most of the surface facts of the Transfiguration accounts, what can we say about its ultimate meaning and what it tells us about God and His plan to be worked out through His Anointed One? First, this is before all a *moment of divine disclosure*. We have already seen that this experience is intended to be a foretaste of the Messiah's divine glory. That glory had been wrapped in flesh for over thirty years. Here that flesh is, one might say, pulled aside for the benefit of the inner circle, and for us, to behold. No wonder John later wrote, "And we beheld His glory" (John 1:14). Matthew related that "His face shone like the sun" (17:2), while Mark and Luke referred to His clothes, that they were "intensely white" (Mark 9:3) and "*became* white *and* gleaming" (Luke 9:29). "Heavenly beings in the Bible are usually shining, radiating light like the sun or the stars, and their clothes, too, are dazzling, unearthly in their splendor (Dan 7:9; Rev 4:4)" (Bauckham, *Who is God*, 100). Let Unitarians recognize that this *moment of divine disclosure* cannot be explained away as simply a profound but still human experience for Jesus.

Further reflection on these two Old Testament worthies reveals that Jesus is simply *not in the same category as Moses and*

Elijah. It would almost be enough credit given to Jesus to consider Him in the same group as these two giants, and perhaps that was what was motivating Peter in his suggestion of three "booths" for the three. But the disappearance of Moses and Elijah in the face of the Father's announcement about listening to His "beloved Son" leaves Jesus alone as the ultimate replacement for all anointed lawgivers and prophets. One might even argue that Jesus could be the anointed king in the line of David, while Moses could serve an anointed Levitical role, with Elijah an anointed prophet. This may be true but the Father's announcement disabuses us even of that idea. "Listen to this one," He says as His Son remains alone in His glory. Even Peter's earlier recognition of Jesus as Messiah, insightful as far as it goes, does not go far enough, for Jesus is God's unique and uniquely beloved Son. "Listen to this one."

There is a darker side to the roles of Moses and Elijah as they are set beside this Messiah. Each of those two Old Testament worthies faced strong opposition and rejection and suffering, and in this way they foreshadowed what was to come for Jesus. But for Him the coming bitter opposition will lead to His being put to death, while Moses and Elijah experienced special departures not normally experienced even by human leaders (Deut 34:1–8; 2 Kings 2:9–14). The Father will soon hand over His beloved Son to mocking, torture, and an excruciating death. Jesus had actually explained this more than a week before, but perhaps it did not really sink in for Peter at that time. So, the Father must say: "Listen to this one." This mesmerizing event comes at the midpoint in Mark's account, when Jesus has begun to teach His disciples about His coming passion and death. Yes, this metamorphosis is a memorable and empowering foretaste of His coming glory, but for now Peter and his comrades need to "listen to this one" and find the grace that this experience provides to follow Him to death on a cross.

Magnificent mosaic in the Basilica of the Transfiguration on Mt Tabor

Luke has an added fact about the roles of Moses and Elijah on this momentous day. "And behold, two men were talking with Him, and they were Moses and Elijah, who, appearing in glory, were speaking of His **departure** which He was about to fulfill at Jerusalem" (Luke 9:30–31). This is the dark thread in an otherwise bright tapestry. That word "departure" is the Greek word *exodos*, familiar to Bible readers as the original Greek title of the second book of the Torah. It simply means "departure." (In modern Greek, *exodos* is the word over the exit door on an Olympic Air passenger plane). While Peter is babbling on about tents, these three are discussing what was going to happen to the Messiah in the months that lie ahead. Whether the focus in this word is on His "departure" by death or on His "departure" to heaven, the details of His suffering and His glory would have been a conversation among those three that we would all love to hear!

I mentioned in an earlier chapter the book by Dale Allison, *The New Moses*. He offers a perceptive and sobering analogy quote at this point (p. 248):

> The transfiguration narrative (Matthew 17) has a remarkable twin of sorts in the account of Jesus' execution (Matthew 27:32–54). In the one, a private epiphany, an exalted Jesus, with garments glistening, stands on a high mountain and is flanked by two religious giants from the past. All is light. In the other, a public spectacle, a humiliated Jesus, whose clothes have been torn from him and divided, is lifted upon a cross and flanked by two common convicted criminals. All is darkness. We have here a pictorial antithetic parallelism, a diptych in which the two plates have similar but different colors.

As we start to approach the end of this exploration of the "Crises of the Christ," it is sobering to look ahead to Allison's description of that future scene at Golgotha. It is also good to look back and see clearly that the Messiah's baptism and transfiguration can serve as a sort of *inclusio*, those proverbial "bookends," to His public ministry before His final passion. In both of these crises, the Father made it abundantly clear both by a spoken word and by a blazing vision that Jesus was His Beloved Son, and that we should listen to Him.

▼

 The commentary by Robert Gundry, *Matthew: A Commentary on His Handbook for a Mixed Church under Persecution*, Second Edition (Eerdmans, 1994), and again Richard Bauckham's *Who is God*, provided invaluable help on this chapter.

O my Messiah, You were humbled but You are now glorified. Let the light of Your glory, gracious Lord, shine upon me and even in my face, so that Your love may illuminate the dark places of my life. Peter and James and John needed to listen to You. I also want to hear Your still, small voice, in my heart and mind. And when I listen, may I obey. Through Jesus in glory I pray. Amen.

Chapter 14

Messiah and the Mystery Man

It may seem surprising to readers at this point in the book to have a chapter that centers around the enigmatic character in Genesis 14 named Melchizedek, the "mystery man." I think the reader, however, will soon recognize the benefit of reflecting on how Jesus the Messiah related to this man, mentioned not only in Genesis and Psalms, but also in the New Testament Book of Hebrews.

"Now observe how great this man was to whom Abraham, the patriarch, gave a tenth of the spoils." Such was the high opinion of the inspired penman to the Hebrews regarding Melchizedek as it is recorded in Heb 7:4. The greatness of this unique individual is matched only by the mystery that surrounds him. Actually very little is recorded about this person and we know very little of what he said. In the historical account of his only appearance (Gen 14:17–24), he uttered merely 28 words in the English text, and the original Hebrew expressed his thoughts concisely in only 14 words.

Like an actor in a cameo role, Melchizedek entered unannounced onto the patriarchal stage of the divine drama of redemption, only to exit just as quickly. Generations of Bible students have raised a number of questions that swirl around his person and role. Who exactly was he? What part does he play in the plan of God for mankind? And, most importantly for us, what is his relationship to Messiah Jesus in the argument of the Book of Hebrews? We will examine three aspects of this "mystery man" as we try to address the following issues: (1) Melchizedek the person; (2) Melchizedek the priest; and (3) Melchizedek the priest-king.

Melchizedek the Person

Hebrews 7:1–3 sums up the account in Genesis 14 and begins to develop Melchizedek's uniqueness.

> For this Melchizedek, king of Salem, priest of the Most High God, who met Abraham as he was returning from the slaughter of the kings and blessed him, to whom also Abraham apportioned a tenth part of all, was first of all, by the translation *of his name*, king of righteousness, and then also king of Salem, which is king of peace. Without father, without mother, without genealogy, having neither beginning of days nor end of life, but made like the Son of God, he remains a priest continually.

Different ideas about the identity of Melchizedek have been offered by interpreters over the years. The authors of the Dead Sea Scrolls viewed Melchizedek as something of a super-angel who would play a special role in end-time events. Later rabbis actually taught that he was Shem, the son of Noah! Neither of these views can be supported by the texts in Genesis and Hebrews. Earlier in Hebrews the author presented Jesus as better than the angels (Heb 1:4–14). If Melchizedek was an angel, and Jesus is better than the angels, why would Jesus be a priest like

Melchizedek? The Shem interpretation suffers from the fact that Heb 7:3 states that no genealogy is recorded for Melchizedek, whereas Genesis 9 and 10 are very clear about Shem's ancestors and descendants.

A more popular interpretation is that Melchizedek was Christ Himself in some special preincarnate form. Thus, he would have been like the Old Testament "angel of the LORD" (e.g., Gen 16:7-11; Exod 3:2; Judg 13:3-21). Proponents of this view point to the language of Heb 7:3: "Without father, without mother, without genealogy, having neither beginning of days nor end of life. . ." There are some serious problems, however, with this idea. Six times the writer of Hebrews cited Ps 110:4 when stating that Jesus is a priest "according to the order of Melchizedek" (5:6, 10; 6:20; 7:11, 17, 21). If Jesus actually **was** Melchizedek, He would not be said to be "according to the order of Melchizedek." Furthermore, language of similarity, not identity, is used to describe the relationship between the two. Hebrews 7:3 states that Melchizedek was "made like the Son of God," not that he actually was the Son of God. Finally, Heb 7:15 states that Jesus is a priest "according to the likeness of Melchizedek," not that he actually was Melchizedek. These verses indicate that Melchizedek was an individual who was a type of Christ, not that he actually was the preincarnate Christ.

Who, then, was Melchizedek? Genesis and Hebrews answer that question plainly. He was a king of Jerusalem who was also a priest of the Most High God. The language of Heb 7:3, "Without father, without mother, without genealogy, having neither beginning of days nor end of life" simply means that no record of his ancestors, his birth, his death, or his descendants is given in Genesis. This absence is very important in a book like Genesis where the ancestry of every important character is carefully given (cf. Gen 5, 11, 49). In this way, he serves as an excellent type of the eternal priesthood of Jesus. All of these suggestions are impossible to reconcile with the argument of Hebrews. Melchizedek was a real, historical king-priest who served as a type of the greater king-priest who was to come, Jesus the Messiah.

Melchizedek the Priest

The discussion about Melchizedek in Hebrews appears in its larger context as part of the argument that Jesus is better than various people and institutions of the Israelite theocracy (the word "better" appears thirteen times in the book). The writer is not saying that the old institutions were bad and that Jesus is good. The point is that in the progress of redemption, each of those important institutions or persons had a special and important function. In Jesus, however, there is a consummation and a completion, compared to those earlier people and things who were preparatory. Thus, Jesus is better than the prophets (1:1–3); the angels (1:4–14); Moses (3:1–4:13); the Levitical priesthood (4:14–7:28); His covenant is better than the Old Covenant (8:1–13); and His sacrifice is better than the Old Testament sacrifices (9:1–10:18).

One of the reasons Jesus is better than the Levitical priests is that His priesthood is based on a different and better priesthood than theirs. They were descended from Levi through Aaron. Jesus' priesthood was based on Melchizedek's priestly order, not Levi's. To establish the superiority of Jesus' Melchizedek priesthood over the Levitical priesthood, the author makes three important points:

1. The Levites paid tithes in Abraham to Melchizedek (Heb 7:4–10). "And, so to speak, through Abraham even Levi, who received tithes, paid tithes, for he was still in the loins of his father when Melchizedek met him" (7:9–10). This type of reasoning may sound strange to modern ears, but it was perfectly common in the rabbinic logic of the time. The solidarity of an ancestral family is strongly taught in the Old Testament. Levi paid tithes to Melchizedek, thus acknowledging his superiority, because Levi

was in Abraham. The writer knew that Levi did not literally pay tithes to Melchizedek. Building on the idea that an ancestor is greater than his descendants, Abraham's action affirmed Melchizedek's superiority even to the Levitical priests themselves.

2. Psalm 110:4 anticipated that a different priestly order would someday supersede the Levitical order (7:11–19). Twice in this passage (7:11, 17), the author referred to Ps 110:4, a statement of Yahweh to David's *Adon*, "You are a priest forever according to the order of Melchizedek." Although the Levitical priests served according to the commandments of the law, the statement in Psalm 110 meant that their priesthood was not the ultimate and final priestly order. One from another tribe (Judah, Heb 7:14) arrived to supersede Levi by the power of His endless life.

3. Jesus was made a priest by a divine oath, not simply by physical birth (7:20–24). Psalm 110:4 begins by declaring, "The LORD has sworn and will not change his mind." The Levitical priests served in their role simply because of their birth into the family of Levi, but Jesus was declared a priest by the very oath of Yahweh. Therefore, His covenant is better than the Levitical covenant because it is based on a Divine oath, not simply on natural birth. It is not that the Levites (or the prophets or Moses, for that matter) were bad. The author declared that as great as these revered persons and institutions were, Jesus is simply better.

The writer's conclusion and application to his readers are summed up with this effective rhetorical flourish: "Therefore He is able also to save forever those who draw near to God through Him, since He always lives to make intercession for them" (Heb 7:25).

Melchizedek the Priest-King

The final characteristic of Melchizedek illustrates the special character of Jesus' Messiahship. Melchizedek was both a priest and a king: "For this Melchizedek, king of Salem, priest of the Most High God…" (Heb 7:1a). His very name Melchizedek literally means "my king is righteous." The name of the city over which he reigned as king, Salem, means "peace" (related to the Hebrew "shalom"). The kings in the Israelite theocracy and the priests were governed by clear regulations set forth in Deut 17:14–20 and 18:1–8. They were, however, separate offices for separate individuals: legitimate Judean kings were from the tribe of Judah while priests were from the tribe of Levi. Therefore, it would be impossible for one person to serve in both roles. When kings did stray into priestly functions, they were reminded sternly of the wrongness of their actions. King Saul (1 Sam 13:5–14) was rebuked for attempting to function as a priest and lost his kingship! King Uzziah (2 Chr 26:16–21) was rebuked for usurping a priestly function and was stricken with leprosy!

One of the reasons for the clear distinction between priests and kings in the Old Testament was that this dual role was reserved for a future individual Israelite, the Messiah. This is made clear in the prophecy of Zech 6:12–13:

> And say to him, "Thus says the LORD of hosts, 'Behold, the man whose name is the Branch: for he shall branch out from his place, and he shall build the temple of the LORD. It is he who shall build the temple of the LORD and shall bear royal honor, and shall sit and rule on his throne. And there shall be a priest on his throne, and the counsel of peace shall be between them both.'"

Zechariah declares that the future Messiah/Branch would unite in His person the previously separate offices of priest and king.

It was necessary, therefore, that Jesus' dual role of Messianic Priest and Messianic King should be based on a different type, one that was not present in the Israelite theocracy. Because

Melchizedek, the priest-king, was not of Israelite ancestry, he was the perfect type of the Messianic Priest-King fulfilled in Jesus, who was "according to the likeness of Melchizedek" (Heb 7:15).

We can answer with confidence, "Yes, I now know how great this man was. Melchizedek was truly unique in his greatness." But the author would have us move beyond the type to the antitype, from the shadow to the fulfillment. In Yeshua Hamashiach—Jesus the Anointed One—we have all that we need for this world and the world to come. He is a unique and living *priest*, able to save us, keep us, and intercede for us. He is also an eternal *king*, to whom we willingly bow and pledge our allegiance of faith. Listen to the admonitions of our author as he urges us on:

> Therefore, since we have a great high priest who has passed through the heavens, Jesus the Son of God, let us take hold of our confession. For we do not have a high priest who cannot sympathize with our weaknesses, but One who has been tempted in all things like *we are, yet* without sin. Therefore let us draw near with confidence to the throne of grace, so that we may receive mercy and find grace to help in time of need (Heb 4:14–16).

In light of this marvelous body of truth about the Messiah-Savior-High Priest, let us, therefore, determine that we will know Him more clearly, that we will love Him more dearly, and that we will follow Him more nearly!

 A recent commentary on Hebrews which gives adequate attention to Melchizedek is *Hebrews: A Commentary for Biblical Preaching and Teaching* by Herbert W. Bateman IV and Steven Smith (Kregel, 2021).

High Priestly Messiah, because the gospel is true, we will rejoice before You when You choose to release Peter from prison in answer to our prayers (Acts 12:5–17), and we will seek no less to delight in You when James is beheaded in prison, even as we ask otherwise (Acts 12:1–2). Our testimony will be, "You have done all things well." So why should we pray? Because You are God and we are not. Why pray? Because You command it, commend it, and commune with us through it. We pray in Your high-priestly and most trustworthy name. Amen.

Adapted from Scotty Smith, *Everyday Prayers* (Baker Books, 2011)

Chapter 15

Messiah Jesus—Should Jews Believe in Him?

"Jews should **not** believe in Jesus, because..."
These were the words emblazoned on the front of a flyer printed by the Hillel Union of Jewish Students and distributed on the Arizona State University campus. A friend sent me the flyer and asked for a response.

The flyer continued:

"Jews should **not** believe in Jesus because:

1. He was to have saved them from their enemies (Luke 1:69–71), which he DIDN'T!
2. He was to have saved them from their sins (Matthew 1:21), which he DIDN'T (John 15:24)!
3. He was to have returned as the reigning King Messiah in **that** same generation (Matthew 16:27–28), which he DIDN'T!
4. He was to have come at **that time** without tarrying (Hebrews 10:37), which he DIDN'T!
5. The true Messiah was to be 'David's Son,' and Jesus WASN'T (Matthew 1:18)!

6. The Servant described in Isaiah 53 (which Christians claim was Jesus) was to have lived a long life and have many children (verse 10), and to have had his share of wealth (verse 12), which Jesus DIDN'T! (He died poor and childless at the age of 33.)

Jews should definitely NOT believe in Jesus! The general picture obtained from an impartial reading of the so called New Testament (not to be confused with the New Covenant described in Jeremiah 31:31–34) is one of a would be prophet who failed to actualize his claims.

The God of Israel still offers the Jewish soul the greatest hope and challenge."

As mentioned above, a Hebrew Christian friend sent this author a copy of the above flyer and asked for my response. I wrote back and told him that some of these "reasons" why Jews should NOT believe in Jesus were the common objections to Jesus as Messiah that have been offered for years. Some of them also reflect the more pro-active approach of the modern anti-missionary movement exemplified in the work of Hasidic Lubavitcher Jewish "missionaries." My reply to my friend was to write a simple flyer and suggest that he have it printed and distributed on that same campus – which he did!

My reply was as follows:

"A Response to the Flyer, 'Jews should not believe in Jesus because...'"

1. *"He was to have saved them from their enemies (Luke 1:69–71), which he DIDN'T!"*

The passage referred to is part of the "song" that the priest Zechariah sang at the birth his son, John (the Baptist). If one reads the entire passage (Luke 1:67–69) it becomes clear that Zechariah did not say that Jesus would deliver the Jewish people of His day from their enemies. What Zechariah specifically said about the Messiah was that He would "… give to His people *the* knowledge of salvation by the forgiveness of their sins" (Luke 1:77). This Jesus actually did when He gave His life as a sacrifice for sins in fulfillment of Isa 53:4–6.

2. *"He was to save them from their sins (Matthew 1:21) which he DIDN'T (Jo. 15:24)!"*

Obviously, forgiveness of sin is based on repentance. The Jewish people who have responded positively to the messianic message of Jesus have repented and been saved from their sins. "He came to what was His own, and those who were His own did not receive Him. But as many as received Him, to them He gave the right to become children of God, *even* to those who believe in His name" (John 1:11–12).

3. *"He was to have returned as the reigning King Messiah in* **that** *same generation (Matthew 16:27-28, which he DIDN'T!"*

Jesus stated in Matt 16:28: "Truly I say to you, there are some of those who are standing here who will not taste death until they see the Son of Man coming in His kingdom." Immediately following this statement, Jesus took Peter, James and John up a mountain where He was "transfigured" before them. Moses and Elijah also appeared with Him "in glory" (see the earlier chapter). This "transfiguration," when Jesus' face shone with unveiled glory, was a foretaste of the future kingdom and was a fulfillment of the promise in Matt 16:28. Some who had been standing there and heard Jesus say those words later saw His glory in the Transfiguration.

4. *"He was to return at that time without delay (Hebrews 10:37), which he DIDN'T!"*

Heb 10:37 does not say that Jesus would come again "at that time," but says: "For yet in a very little while, He who is coming will come, and will not delay." The writer is quoting from the Prophet Habakkuk who had wondered when divine righteousness would be vindicated in light of the suffering he was witnessing. God answered his complaint and told him to be patient and wait for God's plan to be fulfilled (Hab 2:3–4). The writer is simply encouraging his readers with the same message that has encouraged Jewish sufferers throughout the ages: "Be patient and wait for the Lord to accomplish His purpose." As a matter of fact, *Targum Jonathan* paraphrases the Habakkuk passage in this way: "If there is a long period of waiting for the event, keep looking out for it; behold, it will come in its appointed time, and will not be late." The psalmist reminds us that a thousand years in God's sight are as yesterday or as a watch in the night (Ps 90:4). Peter dealt with the same question in 2 Peter 3:3–16. The apparent "delay" in the Lord's coming gives further opportunity for people to accept the message that will prepare them to be spared the awful, apocalyptic events of that future judgment.

5. *"The true Messiah was to be 'David's Son,' and Jesus WASN'T (Matthew 1:18)!"*

The genealogy of Matthew 1 traces the ancestry of Jesus back through David to Abraham by way of His "legal" father, Joseph. This would legally qualify Him as a genuine descendant of David, even though He was not Joseph's "natural" son. For those who may question this, there is also the evidence of Luke 3:23–38 which traces Jesus' descent from David (Luke 3:31) by way of His mother Mary. In light of the rabbinic ruling determining a child's Jewishness by his mother's Jewishness, such evidence cannot be lightly regarded.

6. *"The Servant described in Isaiah 53... was to have lived a long life and have many children (v.10), and to have had his share of*

wealth (v. 12), which Jesus DIDN'T."

Isaiah 53:10 actually reads: "Yet it was the will of the LORD to crush him; he has put him to grief; when his soul makes an offering for sin, he shall see his offspring; he shall prolong his days; the will of the LORD shall prosper in his hand." To become a "sin offering" plainly implies death, and since the Messianic Servant described in Isaiah 53 was to prolong His days *after* becoming a sin offering, it surely refers to life after death, and implies that Messiah must rise from the dead and then live. His "seeing His offspring" was also to follow His becoming a sin offering (dying) first. Therefore, it cannot refer to natural offspring. Jesus was indeed childless as far as natural seed is concerned, but this passage in question does not speak about physical descendants. "His offspring" refers to spiritual seed or followers (notice Ps 22:30: "*Their* seed will serve Him; It will be recounted about the Lord to the *coming* generation"). As to a spiritual seed which was to be the reward of His being a "sin offering," there have been and are to the present day **millions**—those Jews and Gentiles alike who have received Him as their "sin offering."

Regarding the statement that the Servant would have "his share of wealth, which Jesus DIDN'T," it should be noted that Isa 53:12 states that the Servant will "divide him a portion with the many, and he shall divide the spoil with the strong, because he poured out his soul to death and was numbered with the transgressors; yet he bore the sin of many, and makes intercession for the transgressors." The wealth referred to was not physical, but the spiritual reward which the Servant received by His victory over death! This wealth consists of the "many" who were justified (declared righteous) because He had borne their iniquities (Isa 53:11).

(This is the end of my end of my response to that flyer.)

The reader may be struck at the absurdity of many of these Jewish objections to believing in Jesus as Messiah. Sometimes Jewish authors raise legitimate questions – questions that many people of faith, Jewish and Christian, have about their beliefs. Be assured that just as there are answers to skeptics of all persuasions, so there are answers to these and all other objections to the Messianic faith. On a more positive note, I propose some positive affirmations why it is a good and a very wise thing for all people, Jews and Gentiles, to believe in Jesus.

Jews **should** believe in Jesus, because . . .

1. According to Gen 49:10 and Dan 9:25–26, the Messiah had to come during the days of the Second Temple. Jesus was born, ministered, died, and rose again during the latter days of the Temple and even prophesied that it would be destroyed (Matt 24:1–2).

Jews **should** believe in Jesus, because . . .

2. Jesus of Nazareth is the only person in history who fits the portrait of Messiah painted in the Hebrew Scriptures. He was born in Bethlehem (cf. Micah 5:2 and Matt 2:1–6); His birth involved a miracle (cf. Isa 7:14 and Matt 1:18–25); He entered Jerusalem in triumph *and* lowliness (cf. Zech 9:9 and Matt 21:1–9); He was rejected by His own people (cf. Isa 53:1–3 and John 1:11–12); He was tried, condemned, mocked and crucified (cf. Isa 53:7–8; Ps 22:7–17 and Matt 27:1–31); and He died as an innocent sin-bearer for others (cf. Isa 53:5–12 and John 1:29).

Jews **should** believe in Jesus because . . .

3. Of the dozens of "messiahs" that have presented themselves to Israel during the last 1,900 years, only Jesus of Nazareth returned from the dead (Ps 16:10) and has attracted the allegiance of millions of Jewish people beyond His own day.

Jews **should** believe in Jesus because...

4. The God of Israel still offers the Jewish soul the greatest hope, and of Him it is written, "Who has ascended into heaven and descended? Who has gathered the wind in His fists? Who has wrapped the waters in His garment? Who has established all the ends of the earth? What is His name? And what is His Son's name? Surely you know!" (Prov 30:4). His name is "Wonderful Counselor, Mighty God, Everlasting Father, Prince of Peace (Isa 9:6). His name was also "Immanuel" ("God with us"). His personal name was Yeshua or Jesus, meaning "salvation" (Matt 1:21, 23), Israel's greatest Son and mankind's only Savior.

Jesus **should** believe in Jesus because...

5. In doing so, they are being faithful to Abraham, Isaac and Jacob, to the prophets of Israel and to their Biblical heritage. To the praise of God's glory, many Jewish people are believing and are joining their brothers and sisters from the Gentiles who also believe in that "Jewish" Messiah!

▼

 While my Messianic Trilogy, of which this is the "second" volume, addresses many Messianic issues, my book *The Messiah: Revealed, Rejected, Received* (Author House, 2004) interacts also with many Jewish approaches to the vitally important subject of the Messiah.

 Draw me deeper, gracious Lord, into Your purposes and Your plans, so that I may learn to pray effectively for the good things You have in store for me. I also pray for all Jews and Gentiles who do not know Jesus as Messiah. May He fill their hearts with love and draw them to Himself. Through Him I pray. Amen.

A Final Blessing

> Now the God of peace, who brought up from the dead the great Shepherd of the sheep through the blood of the eternal covenant, our Lord Jesus, equip you in every good thing to do His will, by doing in us what is pleasing in His sight, through Jesus the Messiah, to whom *be* the glory forever and ever. Amen (Heb 13:20–21).

Addendum: If this little book finds its way into the hands of a Jewish person who is considering Jesus, please do not hesitate to contact me if you would like to discuss this important matter further. My email address is wvarner@masters.edu. By the way—since this book makes it clear that Jesus is also for the Gentiles, any who are not descendants of Abraham are also more than welcome to write to me!

Further Reading

In the "first" volume of this Messianic Trilogy, Anticipating the Advent, I included an annotated bibliography of recommended works on the issue of Jesus' Messiahship. The following are a few volumes that have appeared since then. This list of suggested reading supplements the books that I mentioned after each chapter.

Abernathy, Andrew and Gregory Goswell. *God's Messiah in the Old Testament: Expectations of a Coming King*. Baker, 2020. Although the authors clearly distance themselves from the approach of John Sailhamer (2021), one of this author's heroes, Abernathy and Goswell thoroughly survey the various Old Testament Messianic prophecies and themes.

Hays, Richard B. *Echoes of Scripture in the Gospels*. Baylor Press, 2016. This treasure was simply overlooked in my earlier bibliography. Readers are in debt to Hays for exploring not just the Messianic connections of the New Testament to the Old Testament, but all the intertextual threads that connect back to the many prophecies, events, and overlooked texts in the First Testament.

Jipp, Joshua W. *The Messianic Theology of the New Testament*. Eerdmans, 2020. As the title conveys, Jipp focuses more on how the New Testament applies the Messianic message than how the Old Testament portrays that theme. He explores the Messianic theme through each Gospel, the Books of Acts, and the later epistles. It could also be titled, A New Testament Biblical Theology of the Messiah.

Williamson, Paul W. and Rita Cefalu, *The Seed of Promise: The Sufferings and Glory of the Messiah*. Glossa House, 2020. The volume contains essays in honor of the Old Testament Scholar, T. Desmond Alexander, who authored The Servant King: The Bible's Portrait of the Messiah (1998). One of the most valuable chapters is the one by James Hamilton, "The Skull Crushing Seed of the Woman: Inner–biblical Interpretation of Genesis 3:15."

www.ingramcontent.com/pod-product-compliance
Lightning Source LLC
Chambersburg PA
CBHW041324110526
44592CB00021B/2815

The Second Time.
1

The Malnourished.
3

The Exposed.
21

The Dehydrated.
37

Those with Preexisting Conditions.
59

The Exile and Refugee.
98

The Convict.
120

What if Someone
169

Takes Advantage of Me?
169

Kinds of Grace.
180

Enemy Love.
184

Works of Mercy.
188

Bio.
1

For Paul, Ardella, the Dominican Friars, and the nuns in south Bay Ridge who hunger.

For my sister and Flint, Michigan and all my Bedouin friends who thirst.

For Will and the undocumented refugee children in my hood who are exposed.

For the exhibitionists across the alley, the wolf, the nudists of Black's Beach, the BDSM crowd, and the underdressed fashion illiterate like me who don't deserve clothes.

For Appleton, Tara, and other diabetics as well as people like my dad whose lifetime of construction and my father-in-law whose living next to Coldwater Creek and its nuclear waste runoff gave them, respectively, cancer.

For the prisoners I know whom I will not name who are guilty, yet who nightly cry out for forgiveness and for a single human presence to grace them from the outside.

For Reverend Kyle Welch, who, after I spent a decade editing books like this and banging my head against a wall with what I've seen behind the curtain of the industry, finally talked me into this genre, for Professor and Reverend Josh Huckabay who kept cheering me on, and for Curtis Roth for the prophetic word — to you and others like you I offer fishes and loaves. Pray he feeds the multitude. Or just one.

For the writers struggling to make time to write: I wrote the full draft of this on my phone, mostly on the toilet while traveling to Little Egypt for baby showers, so I hope it encourages you to find even ten minutes every few days to write whatever God puts on your heart.

And for the rest of us: this book is for we who daily neglect to do something for Jesus.

For Love, our panacea.

Lancelot of Little Egypt
Brooklyn,
New York
&
Sleepy Hollow,
New York
&
Tarrytown,
New York
2021

Jesu juva.

The Second Time.

It unsettles me that Jesus never specified on the second time he said it. The verse fills us with dread in general: where have we overlooked the hungry, the sick, the undocumented refugee or person experiencing homelessness, the naked, the prisoner? When have we neglected to quench, feed, heal, host, and visit? And when — specifically — have we done so to Jesus himself?

The dread grows.

For Jesus, the second time — in the judgment passage, says "the least of these." These what? These who?

These prisoners. These naked. These hungry. These thirsty. These migrants or homeless.

What does he mean by least? And what do *we*?

And do they contradict?

It seems to me there are all kinds of ways to come in last place. And not just the most hungry, most thirsty, most naked, most unhomed, most imprisoned. It's least socially. Least financially. Least in terms of quality of thought or emotional stability. Most lost spiritually. Least attractive. Most obscure. The one who brings the clearest shame. Poorest, most uninfluential, of lowest repute.

It means the one who deserves it the least in every single category.

That. Is wild.